RSPB

POCKET

ARDEN BIRDWATCH

LONDON, NEW YORK,
MUNICH, MELBOURNE, DELHI

Editor Rebecca Warren
Designers Francis Wong, Sonia Barbate
DTP Designer Laragh Kedwell
Production Editor Luca Frassinetti
Production Controller Susanne Worsfold
Managing Editor Sarah Larter
Managing Art Editor Phil Ormerod
Publisher Jonathan Metcalf
Art Director Bryn Walls

**Bird profiles written by Jonathan Elphick
and John Woodward**

First published in 2007 by
Dorling Kindersley Limited
80 Strand, London WC2R 0RL

Copyright © 2007, 2009
Dorling Kindersley Limited
A Penguin Company

2 4 6 8 10 9 7 5 3

A CIP catalogue record for this book
is available from the British Library

ISBN 978-1-4053-4088-5

Colour reproduction by Media Devel
Printing Ltd in the UK
Printed and bound in China by
LEO Paper Products Ltd

Discover more at
www.dk.com

Contents

Introduction 4

About birds 8

Territory 10
Singing 12
Courtship 14
Nesting and rearing 16
Migration 20
Feeding 22
Spring 24
Summer 26
Autumn 28
Winter 30

Birds in your garden 32

The garden habitat 34
Natural food and shelter 36
Types of food 38
Feeders 40
Siting feeders 44
Making food 46
Water 48
Nest boxes 50
Making nest boxes 52

How to identify 54

Anatomy 56
Plumage and markings 58
Size and shape 60
Beak and tail shape 62
Wing shape 64
Watching 66h
Bird profiles 68

The Big Garden Birdwatch 90
Index 94
Acknowledgments 96

Introduction

Gardens are havens for a wide variety of fascinating birds. Any garden, irrespective of its shape, size, or location, can be made attractive to birds, and you may be surprised at how many species will actually visit. Follow the advice in this book and the birds you attract and identify will give you countless hours of enjoyment.

About garden birds

Garden birds include familiar residents such as Robins, Blackbirds, and House Sparrows, as well as summer visitors such as Swifts and House Martins, which fly to the UK from Africa to breed. There are also species that come to the UK for the winter season, including Redwings, Bramblings, and Fieldfares.

More birds than ever before are making use of gardens, resulting in a rise in the number of species classed as garden birds. Woodland birds such as Great Spotted Woodpeckers, Siskins, and Nuthatches have discovered how to make use of the feeders and food provided in gardens.

Garden birds are easier to observe than the more reserved birds of the countryside. If you get to know their daily routine, you'll be able to watch the myriad of changes that occur in the life of a bird. Take care of the birds in your garden by providing food, water, and shelter and you will be rewarded with an endless display of avian activity on your own doorstep.

Feeding station
Supply the right foods and Greenfinches and Blue Tits will become a permanent fixture in your garden. You may even attract species such as Tree Sparrows (upper two birds pictured).

Garden oasis
Providing a source of water will reward you with close-up views of birds bathing and drinking, such as this Woodpigeon.

Bird-garden benefits

Gardens provide a vital habitat for birds. Their value increases with the ongoing loss of the countryside to development. Super-efficient pesticides mean less food for birds, and the loss of hedgerows has deprived them of nesting sites.

Thoughtfully managed, bird-friendly gardens can go some way to compensate for this. Taking steps to help garden birds provides benefits for you as well.

Each season brings new birds and different behaviour to observe. Seeing birds take to a new feeder and watching them raise their young are among the many activities that may take place in your garden. With a little effort, you can make a real contribution to the wellbeing of our bird life.

The bird essentials

You can cater for birds in any garden, whether you live in the middle of a city or in the country-side. It doesn't matter if you have an established garden or whether you are starting from scratch. It is even possible to provide food and nesting sites for birds if you don't have a garden.

All you have to do is remember what birds need, and provide it for them on a regular basis. This is not difficult and does not need to be expensive or time consuming. You can either transform your garden into a wild bird haven, or keep it simple by sticking to the basics – the choice is yours. Birds need four essential things – a regular supply of food and water, a place to nest, and somewhere to roost at night. Provide one, or preferably all, of these things in your garden and birds will come. Each of these four elements will be looked at in more detail later in the book.

A caring community

If you care for the birds in your garden, you are part of a growing community of "bird gardeners". Almost half a million of these take part in the RSPB's Big Garden Bird-watch every January by spending an hour counting the birds in their garden. The enormous amount of data collected by keen garden birdwatchers helps to monitor bird populations all over the country.

Woodland visitor
The Nuthatch (left) is a bird of mature woodland, but providing the right food could attract it into your garden.

Frequent sight
Greenfinches are a year-round sight in gardens, never failing to entertain with their bright colours and comical squabbling at birdfeeders.

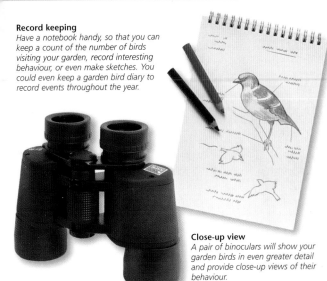

Record keeping

Have a notebook handy, so that you can keep a count of the number of birds visiting your garden, record interesting behaviour, or even make sketches. You could even keep a garden bird diary to record events throughout the year.

Close-up view

A pair of binoculars will show your garden birds in even greater detail and provide close-up views of their behaviour.

Bird profiles

These detailed profiles illustrate 40 regular garden visitors. Each entry gives key information about the bird's characteristics and is illustrated by a photograph of the species in the wild.

About birds

Understanding bird behaviour will give you a greater appreciation of the fascinating lives they lead, from nest building and raising a brood to migration.

Territory

A bird's territory contains everything it needs to survive – food, water, and shelter. Some species, such as Robins and Blackbirds, occupy the same area throughout the year, but most birds have separate territories for the breeding and non-breeding seasons.

Establishing boundaries

Breeding territories must contain enough food for a bird and its mate, plus their young. Males prefer a choice of nesting sites, and need several song posts from which to proclaim the boundaries of their territory and advertise their availability for mating.

Breeding territories are large, and can incorporate several gardens. Some birds may only visit your garden periodically. This is because their territory comprises a network of gardens.

Outside of the breeding season, birds only need to find food for themselves, and can patrol a smaller area. Many species, such as finches, Starlings, and tits, flock together once their breeding season is over – providing added security from predators. Other birds, such as Robins, have a solitary non-breeding territory.

Choosing a home

Finding the ideal home requires a lot of time and effort for a bird, but it is time well spent. Many of the best territories will already be occupied. The challenge is to find one that is

Domestic dispute
There is a hierarchy among tits, but this Blue Tit is making a valiant effort to defend its territory against the larger, more dominant Great Tit.

vacant or make a bid to steal one. Many birds start to search for a breeding territory in late winter to give them ample time to find a mate. Males must choose well – those with the best territories will attract the most female attention.

Musical markers
The male Robin performs a lengthy, varied song to mark the boundaries of its territory.

Non-breeding territories may be selected as early as late summer, when garden birds, including juvenile birds, venture away from their breeding sites.

Territorial defence

Fighting is a common sight during the breeding season. If warning signs such as aggressive posturing and singing fail to deter intruders, territory-holding birds may be forced to get physical.

Chases may end with the birds coming to blows, but don't be concerned if you witness this – it is natural behaviour and the birds are rarely harmed. Disputes outside the breeding season are usually over control of a food source.

Voice of authority
Listen out for the laugh-like "yaffle" call of the Green Woodpecker – a sure sign that a male is patrolling his territory.

Singing

Many species of garden bird have an incredibly varied and musical repertoire – an added incentive to attract birds to your garden. Birdsong escalates in spring as each species adds its distinctive song to the chorus, and the battle for mates and territories commences.

Why birds sing

Watching a bird such as a Song Thrush singing, it is easy to believe it is doing it just for fun. However, singing has a serious purpose. Chiefly a male activity, it is an essential mechanism for attracting a mate and luring females from afar. A good, strong vocal performance is a sign of a healthy male and an attractive mate. Singing is also used for marking and defending territorial boundaries. Song is a very effective way of warning other birds in the area to stay away.

Song and species

Listen to the birds in your garden and you should be able to pick out a variety of different songs – each bird produces its own unique sound. There are many recordings available that will help you learn

Popular song
The Blackbird has a mellow, fluty song. Its simple but melodic sound is a firm favourite with many people.

each species' distinct song. From the explosive trill of the Wren, to the varied repertoire of the Starling – which even includes mimicking telephones and road drills – and the barely audible squeaking of the tiny Goldcrest, with practice you will learn to recognize distinct songs.

Seasonal song

Birdsong becomes increasingly evident in spring. After an initial "tuning up" period during which birds produce a subsong – a muted, disjointed type of song – birds soon find their voices. By late spring, the dawn chorus provides an uplifting start to the day. You can sense each bird's desire to have its voice heard. Autumn and winter are quiet times for birdsong – the voice you are most likely to hear is the wistful warble of the Robin.

Dusk melodies
Birdsong can continue well into the evening, as this Blue Tit illustrates. There is often a resurgence in song at this time, after a break in the middle part of the day.

Late-night performance
The Robin is a common nocturnal singer and is often confused with the Nightingale. At night, Robins regularly choose to sing by street lights.

Courtship

Male birds have to complete many tasks to ensure they breed successfully, and securing a relationship is vital. There are courtship displays to perform and regular bonding activities to undertake before male and female accept one other and begin to rear a family.

Courtship displays

Many birds perform visual displays to make sure they attract the attention of potential mates and rivals. As with songs, different species have distinct styles of display. They may show off their colourful plumage, puff out their feathers to seem larger, or perform elaborate flight displays. Making themselves so obvious carries the risk of being seen by predators, but mating successfully makes the risk worthwhile.

Choosing a partner

Some birds pair only for a single breeding season. Others pair for longer and merely have to renew their bonds every year when they return to the same area to breed. In such cases, courtship is rapid because of this familiarity. Mature, experienced birds make the best parents, and older males are the most skilled at attracting mates. Females consider all of the attributes each prospective male has to offer, but prefer an older mate.

Courtship gift
This male Blue Tit (left) is presenting a female with a gift of food to seal their relationship and prove he is a suitable mate.

Mating dance
During courtship, Dunnocks perform a distinct visual display – shaking their wings while singing – all done in an effort to impress a potential mate.

Preparing to mate

After the initial attraction resulting from singing and displaying, pairs of birds become much closer. The male presents his partner with gifts, in the form of food. This aids the bonding process, but may also prove to the female that he will be a good provider for her during the incubation period and for future young. Mutual preening is another important part of courtship and you can often see pairs of birds preening one another in spring. Once the courting and bonding process is complete, and male and female have accepted each other, and the breeding territory, the pair move on to nesting.

Both birds may become less visible at this point as they do not want to make themselves obvious to predators as they set about raising a family.

Nesting and rearing

The nesting season is a busy time for birds and an exciting time for garden birdwatchers. Breeding successfully is a challenge that every mature bird must rise to every year.

The nesting season

Birds have to reproduce to maintain their numbers and compensate for the inevitable natural losses that occur. Some garden birds can raise as many as four broods in a year.

The nesting season for garden birds lasts from about March to August. Some birds may nest earlier in mild winters. Multi-brooded species, and birds that have suffered a nesting failure may complete their nesting cycle slightly later. Flexibility is the key to coping with the unpredictable weather that occurs in the UK during spring and summer.

Birds nest in this period because there is plenty of natural cover to nest in and an abundance of insect food. The increased daylight hours allow sufficient time to find enough nutrition for the entire family.

Early-nesting bird
Mistle Thrushes are early nesters and this species often builds its nest in the fork of a tree.

Nest construction

Each bird has a unique style of nest and uses different construction materials, which include vegetation, mud, hair, moss, and cobwebs.

Birds nest in a variety of locations, and many garden birds use nest boxes. Some birds build multiple nests and then select the most suitable one to use.

It is vital to select a safe nest site, concealed from predators and sheltered from the elements, as this ensures the best chance of successfully rearing a brood.

In spring, you may see birds gathering beakfuls of grass, vegetation, and mud, which is a sign that they are nesting in, or near, your garden. Assist their efforts by suspending wool and hair from trees, bushes, or a washing line, and maintain a puddle of wet mud in hot, dry weather.

Greenfinch nest
Greenfinches construct their neat, cup-shaped nests in the thickest parts of trees.

Blue Tit nest
Blue Tits build nests in natural cavities such as tree-holes, and also like hole-fronted nest boxes.

Long-tailed Tit nest
Long-tailed Tits make sealed, ball-shaped nests from spiders' webs, moss, and lichens.

Eggs and laying

Once the nest is ready and the pair have mated, the female lays her eggs. She lays one per day because of the strain it places on her body and resources.

A clutch is the total number of eggs laid and incubated at one time, and is dependent on the species. Clutch size also varies within species, depending on the female's condition, food availability, and the weather.

The parent birds incubate the eggs to keep them warm – usually a job for the female. Incubation starts when the clutch is complete so that the eggs hatch at the same time. The incubation period varies between species. Once the eggs have hatched, the adults' work

Nest repairs
A House Sparrow typically builds an untidy nest with materials such as hair and feathers. Nests may need repairs during the season.

intensifies. They have to brood (sit on) the nestlings to keep them warm as chicks cannot maintain their own body temperature, and provide them with food.

The chicks are demanding and need feeding on a very regular basis. Blue Tits make several hundred visits to their nest every day with food to satisfy the appetites of their chicks.

Hatching
Breaking out of an egg is not easy for a tiny chick. A special, hard "egg tooth" on its beak helps the chick smash its way out.

Shell   Egg tooth   Wing

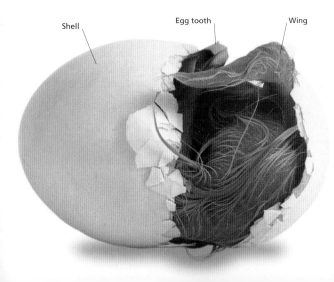

Feeding the nestlings
This female Green Woodpecker is feeding an expectant juvenile. Young birds grow at a rapid pace and must be fed frequently.

Leaving the nest

Parents encourage chicks to leave the nest by bringing them less food. Once chicks are fully grown and fully feathered, they fly the nest and become fledglings.

A fledgling's maiden flight could go smoothly or end in a crash landing. Pride-denting experiences are all part of the learning process for juvenile birds.

Parents still bring food to their young for a time after they have left the nest. Some species learn to fend for themselves very quickly. House Sparrows are independent within a week of leaving the nest, allowing the parents to take a well-deserved rest, or prepare to start a new brood.

ABANDONED BIRDS

Young birds often look lost and vulnerable, but remember that the parents are probably not far away. Fledglings of species such as Robins, Collared Doves, Woodpigeons, and thrushes spend a day or two on the ground before they can fly. In most cases, the birds will be fine, so resist the urge to go to their aid.

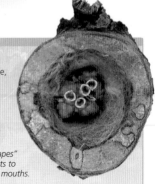

Baby birds
The colourful "gapes" encourage parents to put food in their mouths.

Migration

Birds earn our admiration through their ability to fly. Those that migrate, undergoing incredible, globe-spanning journeys that cover thousands of miles, are truly awe-inspiring. Some birds fly to the UK from as far away as South Africa.

Why they do it

Migration stretches birds to the limits of their endurance and leaves them seriously undernourished. So why do it? Summer visitors migrate to Britain and Europe because of the abundance of food and nesting sites in the northern hemisphere.

Winter visitors migrate to escape the icy, food-deprived environs of northern Europe. Gardens in the UK are sanctuaries for vast numbers of finches and thrushes from Scandinavia and Russian Starlings. Timing is vital for spring arrivals such as Swifts and House Martins.

Mass flight
Millions of Starlings from Eastern Europe and Russia flock to Britain for the winter.

Welcome nourishment
Here a Fieldfare eats windfall fruit, which can be a lifesaver in hard weather. Fieldfares come to the UK in late autumn.

Arrive early and there may not be enough insect food. Arrive late and the best territory will be taken. The benefits of migration outweigh the detriments. It is a risk that many birds have to take to survive.

How they do it

There are many unanswered questions as to how birds migrate with such accuracy. One of the greatest feats of migration is performed by young birds, which instinctively know when to migrate and exactly where to go. To prepare, some species put on as much extra body fat as possible for the journey, without compromising their ability to fly. Regular routes are followed and major landmarks, for example rivers, provide natural markers to guide birds on their way. Once they have reached their destination, birds must replenish the fat supplies used on the journey.

Long-haul flier
The Swallow flies all the way from Africa to feast on insects and nest in barns and outhouses in the UK and Europe. Adults return to the same nesting sites every spring.

Feeding

Feeding is an everyday necessity for birds. Birds will eat both the food you provide for them and food that is naturally available, such as insects. Each species has its own dietary requirements and has adapted to find and eat different foods.

Importance of feeding

In spring, birds endure numerous stresses. Feeding on the right food, and plenty of it, is vital. In summer, natural insect food is ample, but there are extra mouths to feed – providing the right food for adults and young at this time does birds a great service. In autumn, fewer birds will make use of your garden as they take advantage of the

Balancing act
This Blue Tit is using its acrobatic skills and excellent sense of balance to feast on a fallen apple.

Natural food supply
A Song Thrush will turn its head to one side to help spot worms in the soil below before extracting one to eat.

abundance of food available in the countryside. Winter is the most important time to feed garden birds. Natural food is scarce and sudden cold snaps can leave birds tired, hungry, and in need of our help.

Methods of feeding

Every species of garden bird has a particular diet and favoured meal items, and is equipped to find and eat different foods. Beak shape varies by family, from seed-crushing beaks (as with chunky-beaked finches) to insect-catching beaks (as with "tweezer-beaked" Swallows). It is interesting to watch the ways in which different species use their beaks to feed.

Natural foraging

A large percentage of a bird's time is spent searching for food. This uses up valuable energy. Having access to a reliable and large supply of food (such as a well-stocked garden) means that less effort and time is required for foraging.

Some birds search for food over a wide area and may visit several gardens as part of a circuit. Aerial insect eaters, for example Swifts, patrol the same area of sky, snapping up flies in their beaks.

Agile eater
Nuthatches wedge acorns into the bark of trees and use their chisel-like beaks to hammer them open. Their beaks are also used to dig insects out of bark.

HOARDING FOOD

Certain garden birds are excellent hoarders of food. Watch out for Coal Tits and Jays coming to your feeders and flying off with peanuts. This is common behaviour in autumn when they carry off their bounty to secret stashes, which they can call upon during the hard times of winter.

Accidental planters
Jays aid in the regeneration of woodland. Acorns they forget to collect from their underground larders can germinate into oak trees.

■ **SEASONAL TIPS**
*There is much to enjoy
about the garden
in spring, as well
as plenty of "bird
gardening" to
keep you busy.*

1 Food
It is important to provide bird food in spring. It may seem as if the toughest time of winter is over, but a shortage of natural food occurs in March and April.

2 Shelter
Have you provided somewhere for birds to nest? Nest boxes are easy to erect, but you could also provide natural cover in the form of trees and bushes.

3 Cover
Birds are preoccupied with breeding in spring, making them vulnerable to predators. Ensure birdfeeders are placed near cover.

Spring

When spring arrives, there is a buzz of activity in the garden from dawn until dusk. Birdsong fills the air, displays are performed to attract mates, and breeding territories are claimed.

Nesting on their mind

At the start of spring, birds begin to prepare for the most important activity of the year – nesting. Firstly, they have to get into peak condition to meet the physical demands of defending a territory and attracting a mate. Many garden birds take on a fresh new breeding plumage and look more colourful than they did in winter.

Spring arrivals

It is all change in the garden in spring. Some of the birds that spent winter in your garden will disperse to breeding territories elsewhere, while others arrive in spring to breed. Migrants from Africa, such as Swifts and House Martins, begin to appear in gardens in April and May.

VITAL SPRING FOOD

In spring, birds need nutritious food to provide enough energy to complete the many tasks they have at this time of year. Nyjer seeds, sunflower seeds, raisins, and sultanas will all be popular, and very beneficial to birds.

SPRING BIRD PLUMAGE

PIED WAGTAIL
Black and white with long tail

STARLING
Black and speckled with an iridescent sheen

BULLFINCH
Males are red below with a black cap

Noisy neighbour
The "drumming" noise produced by the Great Spotted Woodpecker is created by hammering its strong beak and reinforced skull against a tree.

■ **SEASONAL TIPS**
Summer is a time to care for the new generation of birds that have been born in, or close to, your garden.

1 Predator watch
Young birds start to appear around the garden and "squeak" from flower beds and within bushes – keep cats at bay to help them stay safe.

2 Water
Provide water for your garden birds. Natural supplies dry up in hot summers, and even a small puddle will be gratefully received.

3 Food caution
Young birds can choke on large food items, so make sure everything you put out is in small, manageable pieces that will not swell up inside them.

Summer

We may enjoy relaxing in the garden on summer days, but garden birds are busy tending to the needs of their demanding broods. Young birds are often entertaining to watch.

Baby boom

It is exciting to see the first young birds of the year in your garden, and a relief that birds you have become familiar with have bred successfully. Scaly, short-tailed young Blackbirds are often the first to appear. Female birds that have been missing for weeks will reappear, now that they do not have to brood eggs or young.

Worn out

In contrast to freshly feathered youngsters, adult birds may look scruffy by summer, with worn plumage and missing feathers. They have less time to look after their plumage while tending to their young, so their appearance suffers. Finding food for the young also takes its toll.

A HELPING HAND

Parent birds can struggle to find enough food for their young. Assist their efforts by putting out mealworms or waxworms. Place them in a steep-sided tray and adults will carry the worms to their young, ensuring a nutritious meal.

SUMMER BIRD PLUMAGE

HOUSE MARTIN
White below and glossy blue above

HOUSE SPARROW
Males have a black bib and grey crown

GREENFINCH
Males are green with yellow wing flashes

Colourful visitor
The male Chaffinch is a handsome sight. Provide seed and shrubs and bushes for cover and this finch may become a resident in your garden.

1 Portion control
If you find that a surplus of food remains in your feeders, this is a suitable time to reduce the amount of food you put out for birds.

2 Sanitize
With the breeding season over, you should clean out any nest boxes in your garden with warm, soapy water to prevent the spread of disease.

3 Prepare
Autumn is a good time to purchase and site new feeders. Also, put in any orders for bird food, as the harsh days of winter are quickly approaching.

Autumn

In autumn the breeding season is over, young birds are independent, and birds recuperate from the stresses of the summer. Parents and young go their separate ways, but all are aware that winter is approaching.

Changing times

This is the season when adults moult their old, tatty feathers and replace them with fresh ones. Many birds will go to ground for a time while they do this. They must remain hidden from predators while they are vulnerable. Young birds are moulting too, and start to look more like their parents as they attain adult-like feathers.

Stocking up

It is important for birds to stock up on food while it is easy to find. As autumn progresses, birds gain valuable extra weight. You will also see flocks of birds forming. These gatherings may stay together until the following spring.

THE NATURAL HARVEST

In autumn, food is relatively easy to find in the countryside. Hedgerows are full of berries, orchards have fruit, and wildflowers are setting seed in meadows. Fewer birds may visit your garden at this time, but they will return soon.

AUTUMN BIRD PLUMAGE

GOLDCREST
Yellow crown
White wing bars

GOLDFINCH
Yellow wing bars

COAL TIT
White nape patch and buff below

Autumn colour
Unusual visitors, such as this colourful and unmistakable Jay, may visit your garden in autumn as birds disperse from their place of birth.

1 **Constant supply**
Make sure food and water are always available. Birds cannot afford to waste valuable time and energy visiting an empty garden.

2 **Daily top up**
Fill your feeders and top up your water supplies at the beginning and end of each day, as this is when birds urgently need sustenance.

3 **Ice-free supplies**
Keep your bird tables, feeders, and water supplies free of snow and ice. These can hamper access to vital supplies of food and water.

Winter

Birds face a battle for survival during winter. Days are short and nights are long and cold. Natural food is scarce, so stock your garden with plenty of nutritious food for birds to feed on.

Feeding frenzy

Birds must eat regularly and well to survive in winter. The cold weather is not a problem as feathers provide excellent insulation, but being able to find enough food is the difference between life and death. Birds spend the vast majority of daylight hours feeding to build up sufficient fat reserves to survive the night.

Coming in from the cold

Your resident garden birds will be a regular sight in winter, but you may also spot birds from further afield. Many birds seek sanctuary in gardens as food dwindles in the countryside. You may also spot winter migrants such as Redwings, Fieldfares, Bramblings, and Siskins.

VITAL WINTER FOOD

This is the time to provide birds with high-energy foods such as suet bars, fat balls, and bird cakes laced with nuts, seed, and dried fruit. By the start of winter, much of the natural supply of fruit and berries will have been eaten.

WINTER BIRD PLUMAGE

BLACKCAP

FIELDFARE

Black, white, and orange body

BRAMBLING

Cap is black on males, brown on females

Brown back, speckled below

Winter insulation
This Robin has fluffed its feathers, trapping air for extra warmth. The arrival of hard winter weather brings tough times for our garden birds.

Birds in your garden

There are many simple steps you can take to encourage birds into your garden, such as providing food, water, and nest boxes, and adding bird-friendly plants.

The garden habitat

A well planned garden, managed with birds in mind, is as valuable for birds as parts of the countryside. Provide as many features as you can, from nesting cover to places to feed, and you can create your own private nature reserve.

Gardens are important

It is testimony to the value of gardens as wildlife habitats that so many birds are classed as "garden birds" despite the fact that they are also common residents of the countryside. Many birds seek sanctuary in the form of food and shelter in gardens, where they find respite from the icy grip of winter.

The climate can be unpredictable all year round in the UK and many birds, especially thrushes and finches, come into towns and cities during food shortages and spells of adverse weather.

Gardens also provide nesting sites for birds in spring and summer. Allowing birds access to the roof of your house creates a whole host of extra nesting opportunities. Gardens, and those who own them and cater for birds, provide an invaluable service.

Garden bird sanctuary
This garden is a haven for birds and provides everything they need – food, feeding places, and a variety of plants.

Garden offerings

Almost every garden provides benefits for birds at some stage of the year. Even gardens that are not managed with birds in mind can provide something for the quick-thinking and adaptive species of birds that are able to live alongside us. The smallest things can help birds out, from the seeds formed by a patch of weeds, to a place to nest in an overgrown bush. It is easy to build on such natural attractions and make a garden into a haven for birds all year.

A lawn provides insect eating, ground-feeding birds such as thrushes and Starlings with somewhere to feed. A perimeter hedge is a place to roost and nest, and flowerbeds a place to forage for seeds. Supplementary bird benefits, such as food, bird-baths, and nest boxes, will all add value to a garden.

The more varied you make your garden, the more useful it will be for birds. Aim to include as many natural and supplementary features as possible.

Moveable feast
Earthworms are a great source of food for garden birds. Encourage them by not using pesticides.

Water feature
A pond will provide drinking and bathing places for birds, as well as a home for all kinds of wetland wildlife.

Natural food source
Berry-bearing bushes are a valuable source of food for birds in the autumn and winter. Try to have at least one bush in your garden.

Natural food and shelter

Birds will feel more comfortable coming to your garden if there is cover in which they can perch and fly into to escape predators. Sufficient cover may also attract nesting birds. Native trees, shrubs, and herbaceous plants will add colour to your garden and attract insects for birds to eat.

What to plant

Try to provide some natural cover in your garden. Trees are great, but if you don't have room, you can plant a thick shrub. Privet, ivy, holly, and box plants provide good nesting cover for birds.

Be aware that some trees can grow very tall and have far-spreading roots, so think carefully before planting trees in your garden. It may be best to plant several smaller trees, such as willow, rowan, crab apple, or silver birch rather than a large tree (such as an oak) that may become difficult to manage.

You should make provision for herbaceous plants in your garden. Good bird plants include many

Multi-tasking plants
Plant a nectar-rich flower border like this one to encourage insects. A native wildflower mix will bear seeds for birds.

species that are unfairly dismissed as weeds. Teasel, stinging nettle, ox-eye daisies, verbena, lavender, sunflowers, and thistles all bring benefits to birds through their seeds and the insects they attract.

Effortless bird food
Goldfinches will come to feed on the seedheads of plants such as thistles and teasels.

Fruit and berries

Berries, nuts, and seeds are a popular source of food for birds. Planting a tree or shrub that bears fruit is a sure-fire way to encourage birds. Native species such as hawthorn, elder, blackthorn, and rowan are ideal, but many non-native species

Welcome resource
A tree will provide much for a bird garden – shelter, nesting sites, and food for birds.

BE A MESSY GARDENER
Try not to be too tidy when gardening. Let some grass grow long, and leave a patch of wildflowers – they provide seeds and attract insects for birds to eat. Don't trim back shrubs too early and leave berries intact as a food source throughout winter. Avoid chemical pesticides – birds provide natural pest control.

such as cotoneaster, firethorn (*Pyracantha*) and barberry (*Berberis*) have an attraction to birds. Fruit trees are great too, and thrushes and Starlings will feast upon apples, cherries, and pears and clear up any fallen fruit on the ground. The bird cherry tree provides both insects and fruit for birds, and is an excellent species to plant.

Cold-weather food
The Blackthorn shrub provides nesting sites, and the berries are a source of food for birds in autumn and winter.

Winter favourite
Red berries are an irresistible draw for fruit-loving birds. A cotoneaster will be steadily stripped of its berries by birds.

Types of food

You can buy all kinds of safe and nutritious food for your garden birds. From the most popular individual seeds and specially formulated seed mixes to bird puddings and peanuts, there are a wide variety of tasty treats available for your garden birds.

Meal time favourites

Seed mixes are available for feeders and bird tables. Reputable suppliers offer a wide variety of speciaized mixes, some of which are formulated for specific seasons. Key ingredients include millet, peanut fragments, flaked maize, and suflower seeds. Some mixes include sultanas, raisins, and flaked oats.

Black sunflower seeds are an excellent year-round food. This variety has a higher oil content than the striped seeds, and is more nutritious. Sunflower hearts (the husked kernels) are a popular no-mess food. Pinhead oatmeal is another year-round staple. Also try mealworms and nyjer seed, both of which are very popular with garden birds.

Experiment and see which foods your garden birds prefer. Putting out a variety of foods will increase your chances of attracting more species to your garden.

Nutritious nuts

Unsalted and unroasted peanuts are rich in fats and are an important food to provide in winter and spring. Avoid cheap peanuts, and buy them from a reputable dealer who can guarantee they are safe, for example the RSPB. This is

Garden bird food
A selection of some ready-made foods available are illustrated below and opposite. They are all suitable for garden birds and will help attract a variety of species to your garden.

Mealworms
Mealworms are full of protein and great for baby birds in the breeding season. You can buy dried and live mealworms.

Coconut
Buy a fresh coconut and hang it up after breaking in half. Rinse out the residue of coconut water to prevent mildew.

because some peanuts contain a poison called aflatoxin, which is produced by a soil fungus. Only serve peanuts in wire mesh feeders to ensure small birds don't choke.

Cold weather supplies
When snow covers the ground, supplementary food is a life-saver. Make sure your supplies are well stocked to help birds through these tough times.

Bread
Crumble bread into small pieces and make sure it isn't mouldy. Scatter crumbs in quieter places for shyer species.

Table mix
Seed mixes are ideal for attracting a wide variety of birds to your garden throughout the year.

Glazed seed mix
Glaze coatings bind the seeds together and can provide extra energy for birds. Place on bird tables or in seed trays.

Bird pudding
High-energy bird puddings or cakes come with seeds, berries, peanut fragments, fruit, and insects set in suet.

Feeders

Catering for the varied feeding requirements of garden birds will increase the number of species that visit your garden. Regularly stock your feeders throughout the year and you will be treated to a constant procession of birds coming to feed.

Bird tables

Bird tables are an efficient way of providing food for birds and are a feature of many bird-friendly gardens. A variety of bird table styles and designs are available, but the basic elements are a flat serving area, which should have adequate drainage to prevent food from becoming waterlogged, and raised edges to keep food from blowing away. Bird tables allow several birds to feed simultaneously.

The elevated nature of bird tables protects birds from cats, keeps food off the ground, and allows you to observe garden birds with ease. Birds also feel safe at bird tables because they can see predators approaching.

Low bird table
Both ground-feeding species and birds that also feed at higher levels, such as the Blue Tits and Great Tits shown here, are attracted to low bird tables.

Covered bird table
This pole-mounted bird table has a sturdy base and a roof to keep food dry. The tray is removable for easy cleaning.

Ground feeders

Serving food at ground level is important for those birds that are less comfortable at bird tables and hanging feeders. For example, the Song Thrush and Dunnock are two species that are rare at elevated feeders, but will readily come to food at ground level.

Ground feeders are also excellent for species such as the Wren, which is timid in communal feeding situations.

You can put food directly on the ground and scatter it widely, but it is worth noting that it can spoil quickly and may attract rodents such as rats and squirrels. Specially-designed low bird tables or hoppers solve these potential problems.

Ground-feeder protector
A folding cage placed over a ground feeder protects birds from cats and other predators as they feed.

HYGIENE ALERT

Regularly scrape off old food from bird tables and the ground below. Clean the entire table and the floor beneath it with a mild detergent to prevent droppings and disease accumulating.

Hanging feeders

Birds naturally hang from trees and bushes as they search for food, so coming to a hanging feeder is second nature for many. Several species of bird have enough agility to cling to hanging feeders, while birds that aren't naturally agile, such as Starlings and Robins, have learned how to adapt.

Hanging feeders protect food from rodents and eliminate the risk of a cat attack. Like bird tables, they are a must for any bird garden.

Tubular feeders are perfect for supplying seeds. They usually have several feeding portholes, which have perches for birds to grip onto while they feed.

Mesh feeders are the only safe way to feed peanuts to garden birds, as young birds can choke

HYGIENE ALERT

Keep your birds healthy and prevent disease by cleaning feeders regularly with a mild detergent and a bristle brush. Move your feeders periodically to prevent a build up of droppings.

on whole peanuts. These feeders allow birds to peck off small pieces. Another type of feeder is a hanging cage, which is ideal for bird cake.

Tubular seed feeder
This seed feeder (right) has multiple perches and portholes to allow several birds, in this case Greenfinches and a Great Tit, to feed at once.

Bird-safe peanut feeder
A hanging feeder filled with peanuts will attract a variety of birds, from House Sparrows to Great Spotted Woodpeckers.

Specialist feeders

Squirrels can be an unwelcome visitor to birdfeeders, but there are several innovations to deter them, and stop them from destroying your feeders with their sharp teeth.

Feeder guardians are wire cages that are resistant to squirrel attacks. These can be easily fitted over feeders, allowing small birds to feed. Plastic domed baffles fitted around feeder poles make it difficult for squirrels to get to the food at the top.

There are pole-mounted versions of bird tables and hanging feeders, and you can place seed trays around the poles to prevent food spillage, and

Feeder guardian
The wire cage on this squirrel-proof feeder will deter grey squirrels, but still allow smaller birds, such as these Blue Tits, to come and feed.

give birds an additional feeding station. Special nyjer feeders – which are similar to hanging feeders – may tempt the colourful Goldfinch and other finches into your garden.

Suction-cup window feeder
This feeder will quickly and easily attach to any window, providing an excellent view of birds as they feed.

Siting feeders

Consider the position from which you would like to watch the birds when siting your feeders.

Feeder placement
With a bit of planning, you can position several types of feeder around your garden. If a feeder proves unpopular with the birds, move it around until you find a more suitable site.

Siting feeders

Give careful consideration to the placement of feeders in your garden. You must ensure that birds can find the food easily, but are also safe from predators. You will also want a good view of the feeders, so you can watch the birds without disturbing them. Bear all of these points in mind before you put up a new feeder.

Birds need to have a clear all-round view because they could be taken by surprise by a cat or Sparrowhawk while their minds are occupied with feeding. They also need cover nearby so that they can make a dash for safety if necessary. The ideal scenario is to place bird tables no more than 2–3m from cover.

Bird tables can also be suspended from tree branches via secure chains.

Timid species such as Dunnocks will use low bird tables. Place them close to cover so the birds feel secure.

Wall feeder
Bird tables like this one can be mounted to walls. Make sure they are not too near the roof line where cats or other predators could lurk.

KEY
- [ ] Ground feeders
- [ ] Bird tables
- [ ] Hanging feeders

A caged feeder at ground level is best positioned in an exposed spot so that birds can see predators approaching.

For a good view of the birds coming to your bird table, place it close to your house.

Pole-mounted feeders are easily moved, so find the birds' favoured spot.

Hanging tube feeders can be suspended from tree branches. Ensure threats are minimized.

Easy, natural feeder
Rub food into the cracks of a log, as shown here, to make a rustic feeder.

BIRDFEEDER THREATS

Cats pose one of the biggest threats to the safety of garden birds. They kill millions of birds every year in the UK. You can help to keep the birds in your garden safe by putting careful thought into where you position your feeders and encourage birds to feed. Sonar devices and prickly bushes are good cat deterrents.

Natural predator
Help to alert birds to an approaching cat by fitting a small bell to its quick-release collar.

Making food

You can use your own culinary skills to provide food for birds to complement the specialist bird food you buy. Many of your leftovers will be gratefully accepted by birds, so consider this before you reach for the dustbin.

Making your own bird cake

Give your garden birds a treat and make them a cake. Mix seed, unsalted, chopped peanuts, small pieces of fruit, and kitchen leftovers (see opposite) with melted suet or lard in a saucepan. Fashion the mix into ball shapes, bars, and cakes with the aid of moulds.

Let the cake set and then hang it up on a hook, or place in a cage feeder. Bird cakes are a great way of giving your birds the energy they need to survive in hard weather.

Quick feeder
You can put bird cake mix and suet into the cracks and crevices of hanging logs.

Using your leftovers

Many kitchen scraps provide excellent, nutritious food for garden birds. They are great additions to the bird table and will soon attract a wide variety of birds.

Important items to avoid are salty, spicy, and mouldy foods, unsaturated fats, cooked porridge oats,

Valuable food source
Birds are not too proud or fussy to take advantage of our leftovers. Many garden birds, including Blackbirds, will eat kitchen scraps.

although these are fine raw, and desiccated coconut, which can swell up inside a bird's stomach.

Some of the foods that birds love and that are often thrown away at meal times are illustrated below. All of these are of value to birds, particularly in winter when natural food is hard to find. Supplementing the specialist bird food you buy with kitchen leftovers also helps to keep the costs of your bird garden down, and further varies the diet of your garden birds.

Outdoor dining
This Robin is enjoying some leftover bread. Bird tables are the ideal place to put out scraps such as old vegetables.

Bacon rind
The rind from unsalted bacon and other cuts of meat should be cut into manageable pieces.

Cheese
Stale (but not mouldy) cheese can be grated and put out for birds. It is rich in protein.

Potatoes
Cooked potatoes are a regular leftover, which can be put to good use on the bird table.

Cake
Cake is fine for birds, but only put out small amounts, as it is not particularly nutritious.

Rice
Cooked, unflavoured rice is a popular bird table treat. It is a particular favourite of Starlings.

Fruit
Any fruit that is starting to soften or brown will make a fine meal for birds.

Water

It is easy to concentrate on providing food for birds and forget that water is equally important. Birds need to drink regularly, and keeping their plumage in tip-top condition requires regular baths.

Keeping clean
It is entertaining to watch birds, such as this Jay, take a bath. They are meticulous in their grooming.

Drinking

Birds need access to a clean supply of fresh water throughout the year. Natural supplies can start to run dry in hot summers, and during winter access to fresh water can be blocked by ice. It is especially important to remember to provide water at these times. The birds that you provide food for will also visit your water supply.

Bathing

Keeping feathers free from dust and dirt is important for birds, as it ensures they maintain their ability to fly. Birds must make sure their feathers do not become too wet and render them flightless and vulnerable to predators – to avoid this they flick water over themselves. Birds are communal bathers and you may be able to watch several species bathing together.

How to provide water

A birdbath is an attractive addition to your garden, but you can also place plant pot saucers in the ground or opt for a pond. Ensure birds have an all-round view and use shallow vessels to avoid drowning. Provide only clean, fresh water and change it regularly. Don't use chemicals to clean birdbaths, and defrost them in winter using hot water.

Easy access
Shallow edges enable birds, such as this Greenfinch, to come and drink with their feet still firmly on the ground.

Bathing in safety
An elevated birdbath allows you to watch birds easily and keeps them safe from marauding cats.

Nest boxes

**The easiest way to encourage birds to nest in your garden
is to provide nest boxes. Because natural nesting sites such
as holes in old trees and hedgerows are now less common,
they provide valuable nesting sites for many birds.**

Open nest boxes

There are two main types
of nest box, and each is
used by a different set of
birds. To give yourself the
best chance of attracting
tenants, think about
which birds you currently
see on a regular basis
in, or near, your garden.
 The first major style of
nest box is the open-
fronted variety, which
is either a half-open or
completely open design.
This style is used by Robins, Wrens,
and Spotted Flycatchers, and less
frequently by Blackbirds.

Safe haven
*This simple construction has one half of
the front panel cut away, allowing the
birds to enter and leave with ease.*

Open-fronted boxes are well ventilated and easy to clean. They provide birds with a safe place to raise a brood and to roost.

Closed nest boxes

The hole-fronted nest box is popular with Blue and Great Tits because it mimics the holes in trees that they use as natural nest sites. The size of the entrance hole varies for different species, from a 25mm diameter for Blue Tits, a 45mm opening for Starlings, and up to a 150mm opening for Tawny Owls. Several other species regularly use hole-fronted nest boxes, including Nuthatches, Coal Tits, and House Sparrows.

Classic design
The size of the nest box hole determines which species will nest in it. House Sparrows favour this design.

Other boxes

New nest box innovations include boxes for House Martins, which are placed under the eaves of a house, and internal boxes for Swifts, which can be used in areas such as lofts. Fewer modern buildings allow space for these birds to nest, so you will be doing them a great service if you do erect a box for them.

Sparrow terraces capitalize on the House Sparrow's colonial nature. If you have a large garden with a mature tree, you could put up a tea chest-type box for tawny owls.

Modern design
A removable front panel allows this nest box to be easily cleaned out after the breeding season has ended.

Well-concealed home
This hole-fronted nest box has a 25mm diameter opening to attract Blue Tits, and has been thoughtfully positioned within concealing ivy.

HYGIENE ALERT

Clean your nest boxes from August onwards, once the birds have stopped using them. Discard old nests and use boiling water to kill any remaining parasites. Let the box dry completely before replacing the lid.

Making nest boxes

Making a nest box for your garden is easy, fun, and can be very rewarding. Your efforts will be much appreciated by garden birds, and you will be delighted to discover that a box you have made has been selected and occupied by a family of nesting birds.

Building a home

It is possible to make your own version of both the open-fronted and hole-fronted style of nest box. It is not as difficult as you might think, as shown by the basic plan on the opposite page.

DIY nest box building is also a cheap way of providing valuable nesting sites for your garden birds. The materials you will need are weatherproof wood, galvanized nails and screws, and a hinge or strip of rubber for the lid.

Different bird species require holes of different diameters, for example: 25mm for Blue and Coal tits; 28mm for Great Tits; 32mm for House Sparrows; 45mm for Starlings; and 50mm for Great Spotted Woodpeckers.

The inside wall of the box, below the entrance hole, should have a rough texture to help the young birds to clamber up when it is time for them to leave.

Face the box between north and east to avoid strong sunlight and wet winds, and tilt it slightly forwards to keep the rain off. Hole-fronted boxes should be positioned at a height of 2–4m.

Selective entrance
Open-fronted boxes should be placed at a height of 2–4m for Spotted Flycatchers, and less than 2m high for other species of bird.

Natural home
Your homemade nest box will soon blend in and become part of your garden's natural surroundings (left).

HOW TO BUILD A NEST BOX

Use the dimensions shown to mark and cut the wooden panels. Mark out the entrance hole using a compass and carefully cut it out. The metal plate deters predators. Use 38mm galvanized screws and nails to fix the panels together, and leave the wood used for the box untreated for the safety of the birds.

Materials

❶ 15mm thick floorboard or plywood

❷ Metal plate or tin lid to reinforce the entrance hole

❸ Metal hinge or strip of waterproof material

Fit a hinge to the lid to make cleaning out the box easier. Cut the back of the lid at an angle to fit tightly against the back panel.

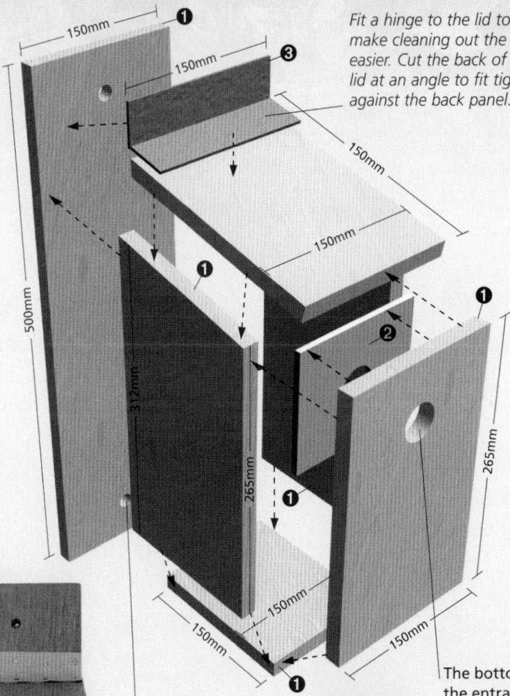

150mm ❶
150mm ❸
150mm
150mm
500mm
312mm
265mm
265mm
150mm ❶
150mm
150mm
❶
❷
❶

Before assembly, drill a small attachment hole at the top and the bottom of the back panel

The bottom of the entrance hole must be at least 125mm from the floor of the box for the birds' safety

Completed nest box
Secure the box to a tree or wall using a screw at the top and another at the bottom. Add catches to the lid for extra security.

Convert to an open nest box
Replace the entrance hole panel with one that covers half of the front.

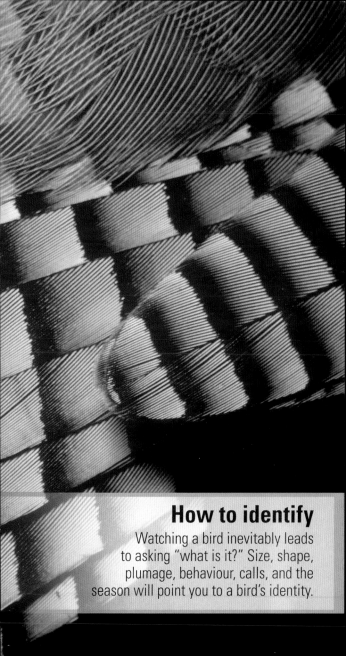

How to identify

Watching a bird inevitably leads to asking "what is it?" Size, shape, plumage, behaviour, calls, and the season will point you to a bird's identity.

Anatomy

Becoming familiar with bird anatomy will hone your identification skills and give you an insight into how our feathered friends function. It will also add to your enjoyment when birdwatching.

Basics of bird anatomy

Birds are brilliantly built for flight, with a strong, lightweight skeleton, a covering of thousands of feathers of a variety of types, and strong muscles and wings. Having a lightweight beak instead of heavy teeth and jawbones also reduces their mass. Many bones in a bird's skeleton are hollow to make them

wing tip

wing

axillary feathers

flanks

primary wing feathers

secondary wing feathers

rump

Flight feathers
Flight feathers, such as the primaries and secondaries, are strong and stiff to enable birds to propel themselves through the air. The same is true of tail feathers, which are used for balance, as well as in flight.

tail

vent

claws

under tail

extra light. A honeycomb structure of struts within the bones adds the necessary strength.

Birds spend much of their time on the ground, and they must be agile on their feet. Garden birds need to be able to perch in trees and bushes, and therefore have strong, gripping feet and toes. Beaks come in numerous shapes and sizes, depending on the bird's diet and feeding style.

The eyes of most birds are on the sides of their head. This is called monocular vision, and its wide field of view allows birds to see any approaching danger quickly.

Feathers

Feathers serve a multitude of useful purposes for birds. They are used for heat conservation, waterproofing, camouflage, display, and flight. The image of the Robin shown here indicates some of the major feather types.

Feathers have a hollow shaft down the middle, with a flat area on each side – the vane. The bare base of the shaft is called the quill. The vane is made up of small side branches linked together by smaller hooked branches, called barbules.

Birds keep their feathers tidy and aerodynamic by "zipping up" the barbules using their beaks, which is why preening is such an important activity for birds.

eye

forehead

beak

chin

throat

breast

belly

feet

Contour feathers
The smaller, fluffy feathers on the body are called contour feathers. They lie flat and give birds their streamlined shape. The downy feathers that lie against the skin have excellent insulating properties.

BIRD SENSES
Owls have incredibly acute hearing and excellent vision. They can turn their heads through around 270°. Their disc-shaped faces are designed to trap and filter sound waves towards an owl's hidden ears. This process allows owls to detect the faint sound of mice and other prey. The Tawny Owl regularly visits gardens, although you are more likely to hear one calling at night than to see it.

Plumage and markings

Feathers give a bird its colours and markings. The plumage of some birds is bright for display, while others are muted, designed for camouflage. Males and females may have different plumages and markings, and young birds pose another identification challenge when they start to appear.

Changing appearances

The males and females of many species of birds are very similar, but in some cases, their appearances are strikingly different. Male and female Robins and Wrens are very hard to tell apart, but the different sexes of Blackbirds and Greenfinches are easy to identify.

Young birds also look very different to their parents. Their first set of feathers is known as juvenile plumage. As the autumn progresses, juvenile birds attain first winter plumage. By this time, most young garden birds are virtually identical to adults.

Birds also change their appearance throughout the year. Some species have a distinct winter or non-breeding plumage. This is usually duller than breeding plumage. In spring, birds moult into a brand new set of feathers, ready for the

Distinctive pattern
The Goldfinch is an easy bird to identify, with its striking red, black, and white face bands and golden wing bars.

FEATHER CARE

Birds must keep their plumage in excellent condition to retain their flying ability. Their daily grooming routine includes preening individual feathers with their beak, using oil from a special preen gland on their back. This ensures the feathers remain waterproof. Old feathers are replaced one by one with new ones during a moult.

breeding season. By late summer, the adults' plumage is worn, so they perform another moult in the autumn, back into winter plumage.

Identifying feathers
As shown here, the individual feathers of birds are very different. With practice you may be able to identify some of the feathers you find in your garden.

and above the eye, wing bars, the pattern of the head, tail bands, and rump patches. The upper-and underparts are often different colours and the latter may be strongly marked, as with the speckling on thrushes.

STARLING   **JAY**

BLACKBIRD

TAWNY OWL

Markings

Many birds have a rich array of different markings in their plumage, from stripes and spots to bars and chevrons. Look carefully at the exact position of these markings on the bird as an aid to identification. Some key areas to look for are stripes through

Male Siskin markings
This male Siskin may be small, but it is beautifully marked. Its plumage is an intricate mix of black, yellow, and green.

Black cap

Yellow bar on wings

Dark streaks on green back

Yellow patch on tail

Size and shape

Garden birds come in an array of shapes and sizes. Familiarizing yourself with the body types of the major garden bird groups is a great start.

Size

When faced with an unfamiliar bird, compare its size with a bird you know well, such as a Blackbird. See if it is smaller, larger, or about the same size. You can also use the size of objects in the garden to help you get an idea of its size.

Young birds may take a while to reach full adult size, and there may be a difference in size between sexes, as with the Sparrowhawk.

Remember that birds fluff up their feathers in cold weather to look bigger, and may appear smaller and sleeker after a bath.

Compare and contrast
Compare the size and shape of mystery birds to common species such as Blackbirds and Blue Tits (below) to help you with identification.

Classic shape
A Robin's plump breast and upright stance make it instantly recognizable, even when its red breast is obscured.

Shape

Each species of bird also has a distinctive shape, with factors such as posture, leg and beak length, and the way it behaves all providing additional information. These clues help you assign a bird to a particular family and narrow down the possibilities when consulting an identification guide.

For example, thrushes are slender and upright, pigeons and doves are plump and small-headed, and tits are small and compact. As with size, it is helpful to compare the shape of a mystery bird with a familiar species. Is it chunkier than a Greenfinch, say, or more slender than a Robin?

Neighbourhood watch
Watch your garden birds regularly and you will get to know their behaviour and body types. Compare them with one another to help with identification.

Small head
Round body
Crouching stance
DUNNOCK

Stocky build
Long tail
HOUSE SPARROW

Small, round head
Plump breast
COLLARED DOVE

Small, flat head
Sharply pointed wings
Shallow, forked tail
SWIFT

Round-tipped tail

Beak and tail shape

There are clues to a bird's identity in its beak and tail shape, so make sure you always look at the front and back ends of the birds you see. Garden birds have a number of different beak shapes depending on what they eat, and display a range of different lengths and shapes of tail.

Beak shape

As you spend time observing birds in your garden and watching them feed, the variety of beak styles will become apparent. With practice, you will be able to identify finches and sparrows from their strong, stubby beaks, tits from their small, short beaks, and warblers by their slender beaks.

These subtle differences can be very useful for identification purposes. A bird's beak can give you many clues as to what it eats,

Balancing act
The Long-tailed Tit's long, narrow tail trails out behind it in flight and helps with balance in trees and bushes. Its tiny beak is designed for eating insects.

and thus which family of birds it belongs to. You should also watch how birds use their beaks. You won't see a Spotted Flycatcher probing its slender insect-catching beak into your lawn because it is an aerial feeder, but Starlings probe their long, slender beaks into the grass like sewing machines.

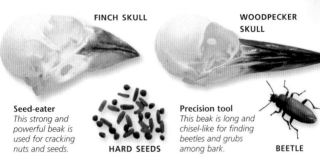

FINCH SKULL

WOODPECKER SKULL

Seed-eater
This strong and powerful beak is used for cracking nuts and seeds.

HARD SEEDS

Precision tool
This beak is long and chisel-like for finding beetles and grubs among bark.

BEETLE

THRUSH SKULL

TAWNY OWL SKULL

Multi-purpose beak
This beak can tackle fruit and all kinds of invertebrates, from worms to snails.

SNAIL SHELL

Meat-eater
This sharp beak has a hooked tip for seizing small mammals and tearing flesh.

MEAT STRIP

Tail shape

Take away the bold black and white colours on a Magpie and its extra-long tail would be its most eye-catching feature. Many garden birds have distinctive tails, so it is always worth trying to ascertain their size and shape.

Look at the very end to see if it is round-tipped, straight-tipped, forked, or adorned with streamers, as with the Swallow. Some birds hold their tails in distinctive ways. Wrens cock theirs and Collared Doves fan theirs as they soar round in display flight.

Feeding the family
The Robin's fine beak shows it is mainly an insect eater. Here, it is packed with insects for its brood.

Wing shape

Many of your sightings of birds will be when they are doing what they do best – flying. Birds have various flight styles, and the more time you spend watching them, the clearer the differences will be. From rapid wingbeats to graceful gliding, each style is unique and a joy to watch.

Wing types

Every bird's wings are made to suit its lifestyle. Swifts spend most of their lives in flight, so they have long, pointed wings to enable them to glide through the air with ease. Migrant birds have long wings in relation to their body, as they have to fly thousands of miles every year. Resident birds such as Wrens and tits have very short wings, as they cover long distances by hopping through bushes and trees.

Seeing a bird in flight is the best way to view its wing type. Check the wingtips – are they sharply pointed or round? You can also get an idea of wing length when you see it perched. Look to see where the wings end in relation to the tail.

Agile flight
Greenfinches have long wings and a dashing, agile flight. In this photograph, one individual is passing food to another.

Flight control

Some birds, such as Swifts and Sparrowhawks, are built for speed, while others, for example Tawny Owls, are built for a silent, stealthy flight in order to surprise their prey. Smaller birds have to beat their wings rapidly to fly, but other larger birds are able to spread their broad wings and use rising pockets of air, called thermals, to glide across the sky with minimum effort. You may see Black-headed Gulls, Rooks, and Jackdaws soaring around over your garden from time to time on hot days. A few birds, including Kestrels, can hover in midair.

Taking wing
Garden birds display a wide range of wing shapes and flight styles, which will become apparent as you observe them.

Rounded wings
Blue tits have short, round wings, which are typical of a bird that doesn't have to fly far.

Pointed wings
Starlings have pointed wings, which gives them an arrow shape in flight. They are amazingly agile in large roosts.

Rapid flight
The Feral Pigeon is a descendent of racing pigeons, so it has pointed wings ideal for fast flight.

WOODPECKER WINGS

Woodpeckers spend most of their lives in the tree-tops and rarely have to fly over long distances. They have short, round wings, which they beat quickly and then glide for a time, giving them a striking undulating flight pattern. This style of flight enables them to be recognized even from far away.

Green Woodpecker wing
Woodpeckers' wings help the birds to balance as they clamber around trees.

Watching

Watching garden birds is entertaining and educational. If you have followed some of the advice in the previous pages about attracting birds to your garden, you will be treated to a regular display of avian activity.

Basic tools

Having made the effort to attract birds to your garden, you will want to be able to reap the benefits. Get good views of the birds in your garden and make sure you don't miss any exciting visitors or fascinating bits of behaviour.

One of the joys of watching birds is that it costs nothing and is easy to do. Anyone, regardless of age or bird expertise, can become a birdwatcher. All you need to enjoy the birds in your garden is your eyes and ears, and some time to devote to watching them.

It is well worth considering investing in a pair of binoculars. This will bring the birds close-up, and help with their identification.

Shy visitor
Views of exciting birds like this Great Spotted Woodpecker are thrilling. This species can be shy, so avoid sudden movements if one visits your feeder.

When to watch

Early morning is a time of great activity for birds with peak feeding, singing, and courtship activity and many birds present. It is well worth getting up early to watch this surge in activity.

Late afternoon provides another peak of activity. Birds prepare for the night with a feeding frenzy and you may see birds going to roost. Flocks of Starlings stream over in autumn and winter, and Swifts spiral into the sky to roost on the wing in summer.

Natural camouflage
Use natural cover, such as trees, to help break up your outline if you are watching birds outdoors.

Getting the best view

Hopefully, you will have already put careful thought into where you have positioned your feeders, bird tables, and nest boxes so that you have a clear view.

If you are watching from inside, through a window, you have the perfect hide as birds will not be able to see your outline. Try to keep noise to a minimum and avoid sudden movements.

The longer a feeder or bird table has been in position, the more comfortable birds will feel using it. They will also become more used to your presence, giving you even better views as they feed.

BIRD SURVEY

As you spend time watching the birds in your garden, you may find you want to keep a record of how many birds are visiting. You will notice differences in numbers at various times of the day, throughout the year, and from year to year, raising all sorts of fascinating questions.

Counting the birds
A clicker is the perfect way to keep a count of the birds in your garden – great for keeping score for the RSPB's Big Garden Birdwatch.

Bird profiles

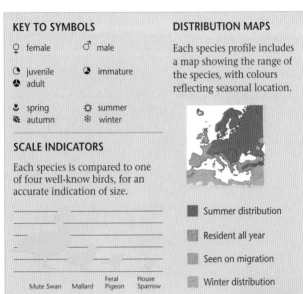

KEY TO SYMBOLS

♀ female   ♂ male

☽ juvenile   ☾ immature
● adult

☘ spring   ☼ summer
❀ autumn   ❄ winter

SCALE INDICATORS

Each species is compared to one
of four well-know birds, for an
accurate indication of size.

Mute Swan   Mallard   Feral Pigeon   House Sparrow

DISTRIBUTION MAPS

Each species profile includes
a map showing the range of
the species, with colours
reflecting seasonal location.

■ Summer distribution

■ Resident all year

■ Seen on migration

■ Winter distribution

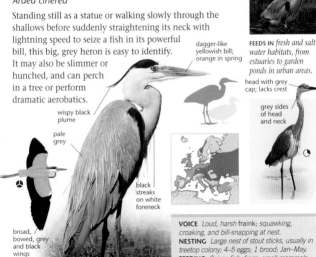

Grey Heron

Ardea cinerea

Standing still as a statue or walking slowly through the
shallows before suddenly straightening its neck with
lightning speed to seize a fish in its powerful
bill, this big, grey heron is easy to identify.
It may also be slimmer or
hunched, and can perch
in a tree or perform
dramatic aerobatics.

dagger-like
yellowish bill;
orange in spring

FEEDS IN *fresh and salt
water habitats, from
estuaries to garden
ponds in urban areas.*

head with grey
cap; lacks crest

wispy black
plume

pale
grey

grey sides
of head
and neck

black
streaks
on white
foreneck

broad,
bowed, grey
and black
wings

long yellowish
legs, reddish
in spring

VOICE *Loud, harsh fraink; squawking,
croaking, and bill-snapping at nest.*
NESTING *Large nest of stout sticks, usually in
treetop colony; 4–5 eggs; 1 brood; Jan–May.*
FEEDING *Seizes fish, frogs, small mammals,
and other prey in its bill, typically after long,
patient stalk before sudden strike.*
SIMILAR SPECIES *Purple Heron.*

Sparrowhawk

Accipiter nisus

HUNTS IN *wide variety of habitats, from dense forests to cities. Breeds in wooded farmland and forest; winters in more open country.*

The Sparrowhawk is a small, quick, agile bird hunter, adapted for pursuing its prey through forests. It has relatively short, broad wings and a long tail, giving it great manoeuvrability. It often dashes into view at low level with a distinctive flap-flap-glide action, then jinks and swerves to disappear through a tight gap. At other times, it soars over the woods on fanned wings, sweeping them back to a point in fast glides. The male, much smaller than the female, is blue-grey above with bright rusty orange below; the female is browner above and whitish barred with grey below.

orange bws

♂

short, small head

broad wings (may be angled back to a point in fast flight)

long, thin, square tail

♀

fine grey bars

glaring yellow eyes gives fierce expression

orange on face

barred orange below

TIP

Sparrowhawks frequently take their prey to regular perches, where they pluck and devour them. These perches are often obvious from the litter of prey remains fallen below.

pale line

darker grey above

browner above

brown bars

grey bars

♀

♂

long, thin, yellow legs

VOICE *Repetitive kek-kek-kek-kek-kek, thin squealing peee-ee, but generally quiet away from nest.*
NESTING *Small, flat platform of thin twigs on flat branch close to tree trunk; 4–5 eggs; 1 brood; Mar–Jun.*
FEEDING *Hunts small birds, darting along hedges, woodland edges, or into gardens to take prey by surprise; males take mainly tits and finches, larger females take thrushes and pigeons.*
SIMILAR SPECIES *Kestrel, Goshawk.*

Rock Dove

Columba livia

The wild ancestor of the town or feral pigeon, the Rock Dove is a bird of rocky coasts and crags. It is paler, with an ash-grey back, a green and purple gloss on its neck, two broad black wingbars, and a white rump. Feral pigeons have very varied plumage patterns, and interbreeding between the two forms has made the genuine wild Rock Dove a rarity.

BREEDS ON *coastal cliffs and mountains. Feral birds widespread from coasts to cities, and on farmland.*

tiny white patch

pale grey back

larger white patch

glossy purple and green on neck

FERAL PIGEON

dark below

white rump

white underwing

two long, broad, black bars on wings

VOICE *Deep, rolling, moaning coo, oo-ooh-oorr, oo-roo-coo.*
NESTING *Loose, untidy, sparse nest on ledge or in cavity; 2 eggs; 3 broods; all year.*
FEEDING *Forages for seeds, buds, berries, and small invertebrates on ground.*
SIMILAR SPECIES *Woodpigeon, Stock Dove,*

Woodpigeon

Columba palumbus

A large, common, boldly marked pigeon, often found in large flocks, the Woodpigeon is usually identifiable by its white neck patch, pink breast, white wingbar, and plump, small-headed look. Although tame in city parks, it is shy in rural areas where it is persecuted as a pest.

FEEDS MAINLY *on farmland; breeds in a variety of woodland and farmland with trees, also town parks and big gardens.*

rump paler than back

bold white neck patch

grey back

dark tail band

large white midwing patch

pink breast

white on wings

no white on neck

dull red legs

duller

broad dark band at end of tail

VOICE *Husky, muffled, repeated cooing, coo-coo-cu, cu-coo, cook; loud wing clatter in sudden take-off; wing claps in display flight.*
NESTING *Thin platform of twigs in tree or bush; 2 eggs; 1–2 broods; Apr–Sep.*
FEEDING *Eats, buds, leaves, berries, and fruit in trees and on ground; visits bird tables.*
SIMILAR SPECIES *Stock Dove, Rock Dove.*

Collared Dove

Streptopelia decaocto

Identifiable by its pale, grey-brown body, its thin, black half-collar, and monotonous triple coo, the Collared Dove is common on farms and in suburbs. It prefers to nest and roost in tall conifers. The male has a dramatic display flight, rising steeply and gliding down in wide arcs on flat wings, with harsh nasal calls.

grey area on upperwings

dark wingtips

white-tipped tail

pale, grey-brown body

black half-collar

pinkish head and breast

no collar

sandy-buff

VOICE *Loud, repeated triple cu-cooo-cuk; also a nasal gwurrrr call in flight.*
NESTING *Small platform of twigs, rubbish; 2 eggs; 2–3 broods (or more); all year.*
FEEDING *Picks grain, seeds, and shoots from ground; often takes seeds from bird tables.*
SIMILAR SPECIES *Turtle Dove, Rock Dove, Kestrel.*

Tawny Owl

Strix aluco

A big-headed, bulky woodland owl that is generally strictly nocturnal, the Tawny Owl is responsible for the hooting and loud *ke-wick* notes often heard after dark. Beautifully camouflaged, it is hard to spot while roosting in the trees unless betrayed by the mobbing of small birds.

large black eyes

obvious facial disc

large, round head

brown back with row of white spots on each side

short wings and tail

pale spots and bars

VOICE *Loud, excited, yapping ke-wick!, long, quavering hoot, hoo hoo-hooo hoo-o-o.*
NESTING *Hole in tree or building, or old stick nest of crow; 2–5 eggs; 1 brood; Apr–Jun.*
FEEDING *Drops down to take rodents, frogs, beetles, and worms; also small roosting birds.*
SIMILAR SPECIES *Long-eared Owl, Eagle Owl, Tengmalm's Owl.*

Green Woodpecker

Picus viridis

LIVES IN *and around broadleaved and mixed woodland, and heathy places with bushes and trees. Feeds on grassy areas with ants.*

Easily detected, especially in spring, by its loud laughing calls, this big, pale woodpecker forages mainly on the ground. A wary feeder, it is often spotted as it flies up and into cover. Adults are mainly bright green with crimson crowns; young birds are mottled.

bright greenish yellow rump

dark wingtips with pale bars

blackish spots and streaks

vivid red cap (in both sexes)

apple-green upperside

red and black moustache; no red in female

black around whitish eye

♂

greenish yellow rump

VOICE *Loud, shrill, bouncing* keu-keu-keuk; *song a descending* kleu-kleu-kleu-keu-keu.
NESTING *Bores nest hole in tree; 5–7 eggs; 1 brood; May–Jul.*
FEEDING *Eats ants, ants' eggs, and larvae, mainly on ground, using long, sticky tongue to probe nests.*
SIMILAR SPECIES *Golden Oriole.*

Great Spotted Woodpecker

Dendrocopos major

The rapid "drum roll" of this bird is a common sound of spring wood-land. The woodpecker itself is often easy to locate, propped on its tail as it hammers at bark or timber. Although similar to the Middle Spotted, it has less red on its head, and more beneath its tail.

red patch on back of head

FEEDS IN *gardens and scrub as well as mature woodland; breeds in both deciduous and conifer woods.*

bright buff below

all-red crown; less on female

bold black and white above

♂

big white shoulder patch

no red

vivid red under tail

♀

VOICE *Explosive* tchik! *fast rattle of alarm; loud, fast, very short drumming.*
NESTING *Bores nest hole in tree trunk or branch; 4–7 eggs; 1 brood; Apr–Jun.*
FEEDING *Digs insects and grubs from bark with strong bill; also eats seeds and berries.*
SIMILAR SPECIES *Middle Spotted*

Pied Wagtail

Motacilla alba

ROOSTS INCLUDE *trees in town centres; the birds feed in car parks, roadsides, and rooftops; also in farmyards, fields, often by water.*

Common throughout Europe, this boldly patterned wagtail occurs in two forms. The darker Pied Wagtail of Britain and Ireland has a black back, dark flanks, and blackish wings, and the White Wagtail of mainland Europe (which also occurs as a passage migrant in spring and autumn in the British Isles) has a pale grey back and rump, and pale flanks. Both occur in a wide variety of habitats, from farmland to urban areas. They chase insects with agile leaps and runs, constantly nodding their heads and bobbing their long tails.

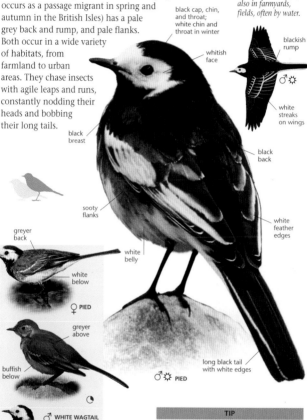

black cap, chin, and throat; white chin and throat in winter

whitish face

blackish rump

♂ ☼

white streaks on wings

black breast

black back

sooty flanks

white feather edges

greyer back

white below

♀ PIED

white belly

greyer above

buffish below

☾

long black tail with white edges

♂ ☼ PIED

♂ WHITE WAGTAIL
M.a.alba

pale grey back and rump

black tail, same as Pied form

TIP

Outside the breeding season Pied and White Wagtails form communal roosts, often with hundreds of birds. These roosts may occur in natural sites such as small trees or reedbeds, but in some areas wagtail roosts can be found on buildings, or even inside large commercial glasshouses, where the birds perch in long lines on the steel cross-beams below the roof.

VOICE *Call loud, musical chrip, chuwee, chrruwee, grading into harder tissik or chiswik; song mixture of these calls and trills.*
NESTING *Grassy cup in cavity in bank, wall, cliff, or woodpile, in outbuilding or under bridge; 5–6 eggs; 2–3 broods; Apr–Aug.*
FEEDING *Feeds very actively on ground, roofs, or waterside mud or rocks, walking, running, leaping up or sideways, or flying in pursuit of flies; also takes other insects, molluscs, and some seeds.*
SIMILAR SPECIES *Grey Wagtail, juvenile Yellow Wagtail.*

Wren

Troglodytes troglodytes

A tiny, plump, finely-barred bird with a surprisingly loud voice, the Wren has a habit of raising its very short tail vertically. It also has a distinctive flight: fast and direct, often plunging straight into dense cover. Wren populations decline in cold winters, but usually recover quite quickly.

SINGS FROM *exposed perches, but more often seen foraging in thick cover at low level, in woods and thickets.*

very slightly downcurved, fine bill

pale stripe over eye

dark barring

short, rounded tail

rusty-brown above with barred wings

faint bars

strong legs and feet

VOICE *Hard, rattling chit, chiti, tzerr; song amazingly loud, fast, warbling with low trill.*
NESTING *Small, loose ball of leaves and grass in bank; 5–6 eggs; 2 broods; Apr–Jul.*
FEEDING *Forages for insects and spiders in low, thick cover, under hedges, in ditches, and other dark, damp places.*
SIMILAR SPECIES *Dunnock, Robin.*

Dunnock

Prunella modularis

Although it is one of many small, streaky, sparrow-like birds, the Dunnock has a fine bill, grey head and breast, and forages on the ground with a distinctive, jerky, creeping shuffle. If disturbed, it generally flies at ground level into the nearest thick bush.

FORAGES FOR *food in low, dense scrub and bushes, on heaths and moors, and in forests, woods, parks, and gardens.*

pale spots on wings

browner head

red-brown eyes

fine, dark bill

grey throat

rich brown with black streaks

orange-brown legs

black-streaked brown wings and back

VOICE *Loud, high, penetrating pseep, vibrant teee; song high, fast warble.*
NESTING *Small grassy cup lined with hair, moss, in bush; 4–5 eggs; 2–3 broods; Apr–Jul.*
FEEDING *Picks small insects and seeds from ground, shuffling under and around bushes.*
SIMILAR SPECIES *Robin, Wren, House Sparrow.*

Robin

Erithacus rubecula

The round-bodied, slim-tailed Robin is a shy, skulking woodland bird over most of its range. It is adapted for following animals such as wild boar and taking small animals from the earth they disturb. In the UK, it follows gardeners instead, and has become very tame.

LIVES IN *open forests and woods, on bushy heaths, and in parks and gardens with hedges and shrubs.*

big black eye

orange-red breast

warm brown above

bluish grey on sides of neck and chest

white breast spot

mottled brown body

VOICE *Sharp* tik, *quick* tik-ik-ik-ik, *high, thin* seep; *song rich, sweet, musical, varied warble.*
NESTING *Domed nest of leaves and grass in bank or bush; 4–6 eggs; 2 broods; Apr–Aug.*
FEEDING *Takes spiders, insects, worms, berries, and seeds, mostly from ground.*
SIMILAR SPECIES *Dunnock, Nightingale, Redstart.*

Blackbird

Turdus merula

A smart, plump thrush with a distinctive habit of raising its tail on landing, the Blackbird is a familiar garden bird. The glossy black male is easy to recognize, but the brown female can be confused with other thrushes despite her darker plumage. Males sing superbly, especially from high perches towards dusk.

LIVES IN *woods with leaf litter, also parks and gardens, and farmland with tall hedges.*

yellow bill and eye-ring

paler wingtips

all-black body

dark brown legs

♂

gingery body

dark bill

dull black
♀ ♂ 1ST ❄

♀ dark brown

mottled below

VOICE *Low, soft* chook, *frequent* pink-pink-pink, *fast alarm rattle, high* srreee; *song superb, musical, varied, full-throated warbling.*
NESTING *Grass and mud cup in shrub or low in tree; 3–5 eggs; 2–4 broods; Mar–Aug.*
FEEDING *Finds worms, insects, and spiders on ground; fruit and berries in bushes.*
SIMILAR SPECIES *Ring Ouzel, Song Thrush.*

Fieldfare

Turdus pilaris

A large, handsome thrush with a striking combination of
plumage colours, the Fieldfare is usually identifiable by its
blue-grey head and white underwing. It is a winter visitor to
most of Europe, like the smaller Redwing, and the two often
feed together in mixed flocks, stripping berries
from fruiting trees and shrubs.

FEEDS ON *farmland,
bushy heaths, woods,
orchards, and gardens
in winter; breeds
in woodland.*

blue-grey head
with black mask

black and
yellow bill

white
under-
wings

dark brown
back

orange-buff breast
with heavy black spots

pale
grey rump

black
tail

whiter
flanks

dense black
chevrons on
white flanks

VOICE *Loud, chuckling chak-chak-chak, low,
nasal weeip; song a rather unmusical mixture
of squeaks, warbles, and whistles.*
NESTING *Cup of grass and twigs in bush or
tree; 5–6 eggs; 1–2 broods; May–Jun.*
FEEDING *Mostly eats worms and insects on
the ground; also fruit from trees and bushes.*
SIMILAR SPECIES *Mistle Thrush, Blackbird.*

Mistle Thrush

Turdus viscivorus

Big, bold, and aggressive, the Mistle Thrush is
the largest of the European thrushes. It has
a tall, long-necked look compared to the
Song Thrush, and often flies much
higher when disturbed. Males often
sing from the tops of tall trees in all
weathers, and in winter
single birds defend
berry-laden trees
against Fieldfares,
Redwings, and
other birds.

bold dark
eye

BREEDS ON *farmland
with tall trees, edges of
moorland near forest,
woodland clearings,
orchards, and parks.*

slender
neck

grey-brown
back

pale outer
coverts

white
underwings

pale
rump

bold black spots
on creamy buff
underside

whitish tail
sides

pale head

pale
spots

VOICE *Loud, rattling chatter, tsairrk-sairr-
sairr-sairk; song repeated wild, fluty phrases.*
NESTING *Loose cup of twigs and grass high
in tree; 3–5 eggs; 2 broods; Mar–Jun.*
FEEDING *Hops on ground, taking seeds and
invertebrates; also eats berries and fruits.*
SIMILAR SPECIES *Song Thrush, Fieldfare,
female Blackbird.*

Song Thrush

Turdus philomelos

Small, pale, and neatly spotted below, the Song Thrush is a familiar bird with a wonderfully vibrant, varied, full-throated song. Well-known for its habit of smashing the shells of snails to extract their soft bodies, it also hauls many earthworms from their burrows. It is declining in many areas, particularly on farmland.

BREEDS AND *feeds in broadleaved woodland, farmland with trees and hedges, parks and gardens with shrubs.*

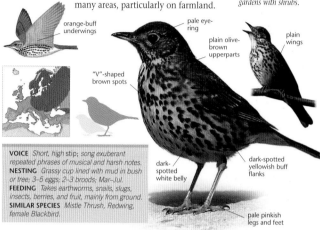

orange-buff underwings

pale eye-ring

plain olive-brown upperparts

plain wings

"V"-shaped brown spots

dark-spotted white belly

dark-spotted yellowish buff flanks

pale pinkish legs and feet

VOICE *Short, high* stip; *song exuberant repeated phrases of musical and harsh notes.*
NESTING *Grassy cup lined with mud in bush or tree; 3–5 eggs; 2–3 broods; Mar–Jul.*
FEEDING *Takes earthworms, snails, slugs, insects, berries, and fruit, mainly from ground.*
SIMILAR SPECIES *Mistle Thrush, Redwing, female Blackbird.*

Redwing

Turdus iliacus

A small, sociable thrush with a bold head pattern and well-defined streaks below, the Redwing is named for its distinctive rusty-red underwings and flanks. It is a winter visitor to much of Europe from the taiga forests of the far north, and typically forages in flocks for berries, often with Fieldfares. In hard winters, it often visits large gardens for food.

FEEDS IN *winter flocks on farmland with hedges, bushy heaths, and gardens.*

bold pale stripe over eye

dark cap

reddish underwing

dark brown back

pale stripe under dark cheeks

short, square tail

dull rust-red flanks

silvery white below, with dark streaks

TIP

On calm, clear autumn nights, migrant Redwings can often be heard flying overhead, calling to each other to stay in contact.

VOICE *Flight call thin, high* seeeh, *also* chuk, chittuk; *song variable repetition of short phrases and chuckling notes.*
NESTING *Cup of grass and twigs, in low bush; 4–6 eggs; 2 broods; Apr–Jul.*
FEEDING *Worms, insects, and seeds taken from ground; berries in winter.*
SIMILAR SPECIES *Song Thrush, Skylark.*

Blackcap

Sylvia atricapilla

The Blackcap is a stocky warbler with a typical, hard, unmusical call. Its song, however, is beautiful, rich, and full-throated, less even than the similar song of the Garden Warbler. It may overwinter in northwest Europe, when it visits gardens to take seeds and scraps, often driving other birds away from feeders.

SINGS *brilliantly from perches in woods, parks, and large bushy gardens, with plenty of thick undergrowth.*

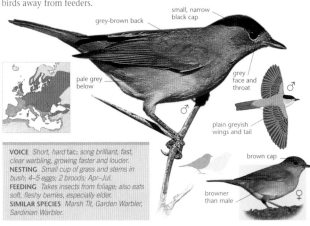

small, narrow black cap

grey-brown back

pale grey below

♂

grey face and throat

♂

plain greyish wings and tail

brown cap

browner than male

♀

VOICE *Short, hard tac; song brilliant, fast, clear warbling, growing faster and louder.*
NESTING *Small cup of grass and stems in bush; 4–5 eggs; 2 broods; Apr–Jul.*
FEEDING *Takes insects from foliage; also eats soft, fleshy berries, especially elder.*
SIMILAR SPECIES *Marsh Tit, Garden Warbler, Sardinian Warbler.*

Chiffchaff

Phylloscopus collybita

By sight the Chiffchaff is almost impossible to distinguish from the Willow Warbler, although the slightly plumper Chiffchaff's habit of dipping its tail downward is a useful clue. When it sings, it betrays its identity by repeating its name over and over again – and luckily it sings a lot, particularly in spring. Some Chiffchaffs spend the winter in western Europe, unlike Willow Warblers.

REPEATS ITS *name from perches in woodland, parks, bushy areas, and large gardens; favours taller trees in summer.*

short, round wings

rounder head than Willow Warbler

white crescent under eye

dips tail while feeding

blackish legs

olive body

VOICE *Call slurred, sweet hweet; song easy, bright chip-chap-chip-chap-chip-chup-chip.*
NESTING *Domed grass nest, low in bush or undergrowth; 5–6 eggs; 1–2 broods; Apr–Jul.*
FEEDING *Takes insects and spiders from leaves, slipping easily through foliage.*
SIMILAR SPECIES *Willow Warbler, Wood Warbler.*

Goldcrest

Regulus regulus

Europe's smallest bird, the agile, busy Goldcrest frequently forages very close to people, apparently oblivious of their presence. This needle-billed, round-bodied bird often gives its high-pitched calls as it searches restlessly for food. It has a plainer face than its close relative, the Firecrest.

FEEDS IN *coniferous and mixed woodland, thickets, and large gardens, throughout the year.*

broad white "V"

olive-green back

blackish wings

yellow inner stripe on black crown

buff below

VOICE *High, sibilant* see-see-see *call; high, fast song,* seedli-ee seedli-ee seedli-ee.
NESTING *Cup of cobwebs and moss, slung from branch; 7–8 eggs; 2 broods; Apr–Jul.*
FEEDING *Picks tiny insects, spiders, and insect eggs from foliage, often hovering briefly.*
SIMILAR SPECIES *Firecrest, Willow Warbler, Chiffchaff.*

Long-tailed Tit

Aegithalos caudatus

The tiny rounded body and slender tail of the Long-tailed Tit give it a ball-and-stick shape that is quite unique among European birds. In summer, family parties move noisily through bushes and undergrowth, but in winter they often travel through woodland in much larger groups, crossing gaps between the trees, one or two at a time.

LIVES IN *woods with bushy undergrowth. Increasingly visits garden feeders.*

pink shoulders

long, black, white-sided tail

black and pink back

black band on white head; all-white in N. race

black and white plumage

dark wings

dull white below

VOICE *High, thin, colourless* seee seee seee; *short, abrupt, low* trrp *or* zerrp.
NESTING *Rounded nest of lichen, moss, cobwebs, and feathers with side entrance, in low bush; 8–12 eggs; 1 brood; Apr–Jun.*
FEEDING *Tiny insects and spiders taken from twigs and foliage; some seeds.*
SIMILAR SPECIES *None.*

Marsh Tit

Parus palustris

Virtually identical to the Willow Tit in its appearance, the slightly slimmer, neater Marsh Tit is most easily identified by its distinctive *pit-chew* call. Despite its name, it is not found in marshes, but prefers mature broadleaved woodland where it often feeds at low level among thick undergrowth.

glossy black cap and back of neck

FORAGES AMONG *tall deciduous trees in woodland and parks, especially beech and oak; also in gardens.*

black bib, smaller than Willow Tit's

neck slimmer than Willow Tit's

pale grey-buff underside

neat, plain grey-brown upperparts

rounded grey-brown wings

VOICE *Bright* pit-chew! *and* titi-zee-zee-zee; *song rippling* schip-schip-schip-schip.
NESTING *Grass and moss cup in pre-existing tree hole; 6–8 eggs, 1 brood; Apr–Jun.*
FEEDING *Mostly insects and spiders in summer; seeds, berries, and nuts in winter.*
SIMILAR SPECIES *Willow Tit, Coal Tit, Blackcap.*

Coal tit

Parus ater

Although often seen in gardens, the diminutive white-naped Coal Tit is typically a bird of conifer trees, where it makes the most of its minute weight by searching the thinnest twigs for food. Active and fearless, it often joins up with other species of tits in autumn and winter, roaming through woodlands

FORAGES AMONG *pines and other conifers; also feeds in low shrubs and visits garden bird feeders.*

yellower cheek

black head

white nape patch

greyish back

dark wings with two white bars

bright buff underside

black bib

white cheek

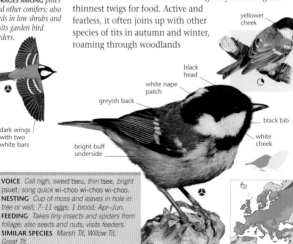

VOICE *Call high, sweet* tseu, *thin* tsee, *bright* psuet; *song quick* wi-choo wi-choo wi-choo.
NESTING *Cup of moss and leaves in hole in tree or wall; 7–11 eggs; 1 brood; Apr–Jun.*
FEEDING *Takes tiny insects and spiders from foliage; also seeds and nuts; visits feeders.*
SIMILAR SPECIES *Marsh Tit, Willow Tit, Great Tit.*

VISITS GARDENS *to feed from nut baskets and other feeders. Lives in woods of all kinds, as well as parks, gardens, and bushy places.*

Blue Tit

Parus caeruleus

Colourful, tame, and noisy, the Blue Tit is mainly yellow and greenish as well as blue. It is a common visitor to bird feeders where its acrobatic skills make it a favourite garden bird. Its black-and-white face pattern is distinctive. A thin, dark central streak often shows on its yellow underside.

bright blue cap

white bars on blue wings

yellow below

blue tail

greenish cap

less blue

VOICE *Thin, quick* tsee-tsee-tsee, *scolding* churrr; *song trilled* tsee-tsee-tsee-tsisisisisisi.
NESTING *Small cup of moss and hair in tree hole/nest box; 7–16 eggs; 1 brood; Apr–May.*
FEEDING *Mainly seeds, nuts, insects, and spiders; often visits garden feeders.*
SIMILAR SPECIES *Coal Tit, Great Tit, Goldcrest.*

BREEDS AND *feeds in wide variety of mixed woodland, as well as parks and gardens. Often uses nest boxes.*

Great Tit

Parus major

The bold, even aggressive Great Tit is one of the most familiar garden and woodland birds. Its calls can be confusing, but it is easily identified by the broad black stripe on its yellow breast. Less agile than the smaller tits, it feeds on the ground more often.

white cheek

green back

shiny black cap

bright yellow underparts with broad black band

yellow cheeks

pale wingbar

band narrower than male

VOICE *Varied calls include ringing* chink *and piping* tui tui tui; *song repeated two-note* tea-cher tea-cher *or* see-too see-too.
NESTING *Cup of moss, leaves, and grass in tree hole; 5–11 eggs; 1 brood; Apr–May.*
FEEDING *Insects, seeds, nuts, especially tree seeds in autumn, winter; often visits feeders.*
SIMILAR SPECIES *Blue Tit, Coal Tit.*

Nuthatch

FORAGES HIGH *in trees and on the ground in deciduous and mixed woodland, parkland, and large gardens, all year round.*

Sitta europaea

Identified by its blue-grey and buff plumage and oddly top-heavy look, the Nuthatch is an agile climber that (unlike other birds) often descends trees head-first, as well as climbing upwards. It wedges nuts and seeds in bark so it can crack them open, with loud blows of its long, grey, chisel-like bill.

broad blue-grey wings

buff below, with rusty flanks

strong feet for clinging to bark

acrobatic pose

black stripe

dagger-like grey bill

short tail

VOICE *Loud, liquid whistles, pew pew pew, chwee chwee; fast ringing trills, loud chwit.*
NESTING *Typically plasters mud around old woodpecker hole lined with bark and leaves; 6–9 eggs; 1 brood; Apr–Jul.*
FEEDING *Variety of seeds, berries, and nuts, often wedged in bark for easy cracking.*
SIMILAR SPECIES *Rock Nuthatch (rare).*

Jay

Garrulus glandarius

Noisy but shy, the Jay often keeps to thick cover and beats a swift retreat if disturbed, flying off with a flash of its bold white rump. It has a curious habit of allowing ants to run over its plumage, probably to employ the ants' chemical defences against parasites.

BREEDS IN *woodland and parks, especially with oak trees, and visits gardens.*

moustache thick and black

pinkish grey body

barred blue wing panel

"anting" posture

raised crest

white patch on black wings

white rump

white under tail

black tail

VOICE *Nasal, mewing pee-oo, short bark; loud, harsh, cloth-tearing skairk!*
NESTING *Bulky stick nest, low in dense bush; 4–5 eggs; 1 brood; Apr–Jun.*
FEEDING *Eats mainly insects in summer, with some eggs and nestlings; stores acorns in autumn for use in winter.*
SIMILAR SPECIES *Hoopoe.*

Magpie

Pica pica

BREEDS ON *farmland with hedges, woodland edges, and urban parks. Visits gardens to find food.*

A handsome crow with boldly pied plumage and a long, tapered tail, the Magpie is unmistakable. In sunlight it has an iridescent sheen of blue, purple, and green. It has a reputation for wiping out songbirds, but research shows that its fondness for eating eggs and chicks has little overall effect on populations.

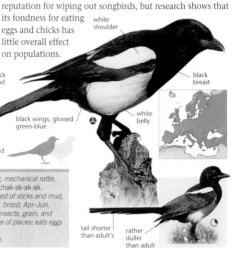

wedge-shaped tail

black head

black lines on white wingtips

black wings, glossed green-blue

long black tail, glossed green and bronze-purple

white shoulder

black breast

white belly

tail shorter than adult's

rather duller than adult

VOICE *Hard, chattering, mechanical rattle, tcha-tcha-tcha-tcha or chak-ak-ak-ak.*
NESTING *Big domed nest of sticks and mud, high in tree; 5–8 eggs; 1 brood; Apr–Jun.*
FEEDING *Mostly takes insects, grain, and scraps from a wide range of places; eats eggs and chicks in summer.*
SIMILAR SPECIES *None.*

Jackdaw

Corvus monedula

LIVES AROUND *cliffs, quarries, old buildings, woods, farmland with mature trees, or towns and villages where there are old houses with chimneys.*

A small, short-billed crow with a black cap and a pale grey nape, the Jackdaw is a very sociable bird that often flies in flocks, performing spectacular aerobatics with much calling. It also feeds in mixed flocks with Rooks, when its compact shape becomes obvious.

grey nape

pale eyes

black cap

grey-black body

rounded wings

short, thick bill

dark grey underwings

VOICE *Noisy kyak or tjak! with squeaky, bright quality; some longer calls like chee-ar.*
NESTING *Pile of sticks lined with mud, moss, and hair, in hole in tree, cliff, or building, or in chimney; 4–6 eggs; 1 brood; Apr–Jul.*
FEEDING *Takes worms, seeds, and scraps from ground; also caterpillars and berries.*
SIMILAR SPECIES *Rook, Chough.*

TIP

Although similar to other black crows such as the Rook, the Jackdaw is distinctly smaller, with shorter legs and a shorter bill.

Rook

Corvus frugilegus

This intensely social crow is known for its loud cawing calls. Adult Rooks are distinguished by a bare, parchment-white face. It has a peaked, rather than flat-topped crown, and ragged thigh feathers create a "baggy trouser" effect.

BREEDS IN *treetop colonies, typically in farmland, parks, and villages or small towns with scattered tall trees for nesting.*

black bill base

bill thinner than Crow's

glossy black body

body deeper, less sleek than Carrion Crow's

looser feathers and slighter body than Crow

loose, ragged thigh feathers

rounded tail

wings more pointed than Carrion Crow's

narrow, rounded tail

VOICE *Raucous, but relaxed cawing, caaar, grah-gra-gra, plus higher, strangled notes.*
NESTING *Big nest of sticks lined with grass, moss, and leaves, in treetop colony; 3–6 eggs; 1 brood; Mar–Jun.*
FEEDING *Eats insects, seeds, grain, and roots from ground; also forages for roadkill.*
SIMILAR SPECIES *Carrion Crow, Jackdaw, Raven.*

Carrion Crow

Corvus corone

The all-black Carrion Crow is easy to confuse with other crows, particularly a juvenile Rook, but its head has a distinctly flatter crown and its body plumage is much tighter and neater-looking, with no "baggy trouser" effect. It is usually seen alone or in pairs, but may gather to feed and roost in flocks in autumn and winter, and often feeds alongside other crows.

LIVES IN *open areas, from farmland to city centres; also feeds on coasts and estuaries.*

thick, arched bill

flat-topped head

squarer wingtips than Rook

glossy black body

neat, tight body feathering

square tail

VOICE *Loud, harsh, grating caw, krra krra krra, metallic konk, korr, and similar calls.*
NESTING *Big stick nest, in tree, bush, on cliff or building; 4–6 eggs; 1 brood; Mar–Jul.*
FEEDING *Feeds on ground, taking all kinds of invertebrates, eggs, grain, and various scraps; usually in pairs but sometimes flocks.*
SIMILAR SPECIES *Rook, Raven, Jackdaw.*

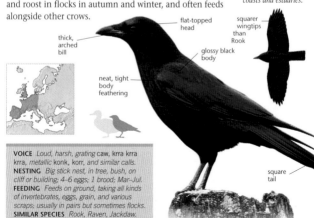

Starling

Sturnus vulgaris

GATHERS IN *big winter flocks in forests, city centres, industrial sites, bridges, and piers. Breeds in woods, gardens, and towns.*

A common, active, noisy, sociable, but quarrelsome bird of urban and rural habitats, the Starling is instantly recognizable by its strong-legged walk and waddling run as it pokes and pries in the soil for insect grubs and seeds. Superficially black, its plumage is glossed with iridescent green and purple in summer, and spotted with buff in winter. Outside the breeding season it forms dense flocks that roost in trees, reedbeds, and on buildings, and swirl around the sky in perfectly co-ordinated aerobatic manoeuvres, particularly at dusk. These winter flocks can be so vast that they look like clouds of smoke at a distance, although declines in many areas have made such immense gatherings less common.

TIP

Starlings are skilled mimics and can even imitate noises such as telephones. A strange sound coming from an odd place often turns out to be a Starling.

short, squarish tail

sharp yellow bill

blue-grey bill base; pale pink on female

glossy black body with green and purple sheen

long, strong, red-brown legs

♂ ♣

silvery face with dark mask

body feathers tipped buff or whitish

feathers edged bright orange-buff

large spots near tail

♠ ❄

dull head last to get adult colours

♣ ⚒ **MOULTING**

plain brown body

dark bill

☾

VOICE *Loud, slightly grating* cheer, *musical, twangy, whistled* tswee-oo, *variety of clicks, gurgles, squawking notes; song fast mixture of rattles, trills, gurgles, and whistles, often with mimicry of other birds or sounds.*
NESTING *Loose, bulky nest of grass and stems, in tree hole, cavity in wall or building, or large nest box; 4–7 eggs; 1–2 broods; Apr–Jul.*
FEEDING *Forages for invertebrates, seeds, and berries on the ground, in small to large flocks; catches flying ants in mid-air.*
SIMILAR SPECIES *Spotless Starling, Blackbird.*

House Sparrow

Passer domesticus

This common, noisy sparrow is one of the most familiar small birds due to its habit of nesting in buildings. The male has a bold black bib and distinctive grey cap, but the female can be confused with a female finch. Although House Sparrow populations have declined, they are still widespread.

LIVES IN *cities, towns, villages, farms, and on farmland; rarely found far from human habitation.*

grey cap

big black bib

red-brown above, with dark streaks

unmarked grey below

whitish wingbar ♂

greyish rump

♂☼

pale stripe

plain plumage

♀

VOICE *Lively chirrup, chilp, as loud chorus from flock; song a simple series of chirps.*
NESTING *Untidy nest of grass and feathers in cavity; 3–7 eggs; 1–4 broods; Apr–Aug.*
FEEDING *Takes seeds, nuts, and berries, mainly from ground, plus insects for young.*
SIMILAR SPECIES *Spanish Sparrow, female Chaffinch.*

Chaffinch

Fringilla coelebs

One of the least specialized of the finches, the Chaffinch is also one of the most successful and abundant. Unusually for finches, pairs breed in separate territories, proclaimed by males singing loudly from prominent perches. At other times they are social and often very tame.

BREEDS IN *coniferous and deciduous forests, woods, hedges, parks, and gardens.*

blue-grey head and bill

brownish pink cheeks and throat

brown back

two bold white wingbars

greenish rump

♂☼

ochre-brown smudges on head

♂❅

dark wings

yellowish feather edges

pink below, whiter on belly

♂☼

olive head and back

♀

dark tail with white sides

VOICE *Soft chup, frequent pink! loud hweet; song chip-chip, chirichiri cheep-tcheweeoo.*
NESTING *Nest neat cup of grass, leaves, and moss, in tree; 4–5 eggs; 1 brood; Apr–May.*
FEEDING *Eats insects, mostly caterpillars, in summer; otherwise seeds, shoots, and berries.*
SIMILAR SPECIES *Brambling, Bullfinch, female House Sparrow.*

Brambling

Fringilla montifringilla

FEEDS IN *farmland and parks, in winter, especially areas with beech, birch, and spruce; breeds in northern forests.*

Very like the Chaffinch, but with a white rump and a darker back, the Brambling is generally less common and very scarce in Europe in summer. In winter, Bramblings may gather in huge feeding flocks, especially in central Europe, but numbers fluctuate from year to year with the supply of beech-mast and other tree seeds.

white rump

big orange-buff upper wingbar

black head and back

♂☼

"scaly" head

bright yellow-orange breast and shoulder

dark back

duller

♀❄

pale throat

white belly

dark spots on flanks

♂❄

VOICE Call hard chek, *distinctive nasal* tsweek; song repeated nasal, buzzing dzeeee.
NESTING Cup of lichen, bark, and stems, in tree or bush; 5–7 eggs; 1 brood; May–Jun.
FEEDING Eats insects in summer, seeds at other times; takes beech-mast from ground.
SIMILAR SPECIES Chaffinch, female House Sparrow.

Goldfinch

Carduelis carduelis

Flocks of colourful Goldfinches feed on waste ground, farmyards, and field edges, picking soft, milky seeds from thistles, tall daisies, and similar plants with their pointed bills. They are agile feeders, often swinging head-down from seedheads, and have a distinctive dancing flight and tinkling calls.

FORAGES IN *weedy places with tall seed-bearing flowers such as thistles and teasels; also in alder and larch.*

bold black, red, and white head

tawny back

yellow on closed wing

tawny-chestnut patch

black wings

pale underside

big yellow panels

grey head

duller wings

VOICE Call chattering, lilting skip-i-lip, rough tschair; song mix of call notes and liquid trills.
NESTING Neat nest of roots, grass, cobwebs in tree or bush; 5–6 eggs; 2 broods; May–Jul.
FEEDING Gathers soft, half-ripe seeds from thistles and similar plants, less often from ground; also eats seeds of alder and larch.
SIMILAR SPECIES Siskin, Greenfinch.

TIP
At a distance the red face can be hard to see, but the yellow wing flashes and bouncy flight action usually make identification easy.

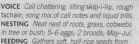

Greenfinch

Carduelis chloris

dark patch

Males are easy to identify by their green plumage with bright yellow flashes, and a "frowning" look; the duller females and juveniles are also stocky and stout-billed, but trickier to distinguish. In spring, males sing during circling, stiff-winged display flights.

FEEDS ON *sunflower seeds at garden feeders; breeds in open woods, hedges, large gardens.*

bright olive green
yellow stripe

♂☼

browner than adult

streaked all over

greyer above

duller than male ♀

♂❄

VOICE *Flight call fast, tinny chatter, tit-it-it-it, nasal dzoo-ee, hard jup-jup-jup; song series of rich trills, mixed with buzzy dzweee.*
NESTING *Bulky nest of grass and twigs in tree; 4–6 eggs; 1–2 broods; Apr–Jul.*
FEEDING *Takes seeds from trees, herbs, and ground; also berries and nuts.*
SIMILAR SPECIES *Citril Finch, Serin, Siskin.*

yellow patches on tail

♂

flashes of yellow on outer part of grey wings

Siskin

Carduelis spinus

A specialist at feeding on tree seeds, the neat, slender Siskin is particularly associated with conifers such as pines and spruces. It usually feeds high in the trees, displaying tit-like agility, and in spring the males often sing from treetops. In winter, Siskins forage in flocks, often with Redpolls.

VISITS GARDENS *for peanuts, but breeds in spruce and pine forest. More widespread in winter.*

black cap and chin

dark streaks on green back

yellow patch each side of black tail

♂

lime-green to yellowish breast

♂

bold yellow wingbars

greyer head than male

like greyer female

♀

VOICE *Whistled tsy-zee; hoarse purr; song mixes calls with trills and hard twittering notes.*
NESTING *Tiny nest of twigs and stems, lined with down, high in tree; 4–5 eggs; 1–2 broods; May–Jul.*
FEEDING *Eats the seeds of pine, larch, alder, birch, and various other trees.*
SIMILAR SPECIES *Greenfinch, Redpoll, Serin.*

Bullfinch

Pyrrhula pyrrhula

Heavily-built, rather sluggish, and often hard to see as it feeds quietly in dense cover, the Bullfinch is unmistakable when it emerges into the open. The male is a striking sight, with his bold red, grey, and black plumage and bright white rump. Generally shy, its caution may be warranted, because it is often treated as a pest due to its taste for soft buds of fruit trees. It is seriously declining in some regions.

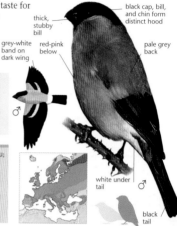

RAIDS FLOWERING *fruit trees in woodland, farmland with hedges, thickets, orchards, parks, and gardens.*

no dark cap
plumage like female
dull brownish back
beige-grey below
♀
grey-white band on dark wing
red-pink below
♂
black cap, bill, and chin form distinct hood
pale grey back
thick, stubby bill
white under tail
♂
black tail

VOICE *Call low, clear whistles, peuuw or phiu; song infrequent, warble mixed with calls.*
NESTING *Cup of twigs, lined with moss and grass, in dense bush or tree; 4–5 eggs, 2 broods, Apr–Jun.*
FEEDING *Eats soft buds, seeds, berries, and shoots from bushes, shrubs, and fruit trees.*
SIMILAR SPECIES *Chaffinch, Jay (far larger).*

Reed Bunting

Emberiza schoeniclus

Easy to find and identify in summer, male Reed Buntings sing monotonously from low perches among reeds and other wetland vegetation. In winter, when the males are far less striking, they are harder to recognize – especially when feeding on farmland or even in gardens.

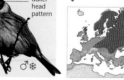

LIVES IN *wet places with reeds, sedge, rushes; also gardens in winter.*

hint of pale collar
♀
cream and black streaks on back
long, notched tail

black head
white collar and moustache
rufous forewing
♂☼
bold white tail sides
duller head pattern
♂☼
brown back with black streaks

streaked, whitish underside
♂☼
pale red-brown legs
black tail with broad white sides

VOICE *Call loud high tseeu, and high, thin, pure swee, zi zi; song short, jangly phrase, srip srip srip sea-sea-sea stitip-itip-itipip.*
NESTING *Bulky nest of grass and sedge, on ground in cover; 4–5 eggs; 2 broods; Apr–Jun.*
FEEDING *Eats seeds, plus insects in summer.*
SIMILAR SPECIES *Female Chaffinch, Female Lapland Bunting, House Sparrow.*

The Big Garden Birdwatch

After reading this book, you will hopefully become a lifelong fan of garden birds, and devote some time to caring for them. Read on to find out how to take part in the world's biggest survey of bird species – the Big Garden Birdwatch and discover more about the RSPB and other ways you can help and enjoy wild birds.

The RSPB's Big Garden Birdwatch takes place annually during the last weekend in January. From humble beginnings in the winter of 1978–79 when it was an activity for the Society's junior membership – then called The Young Ornithologists' Club – the basic principle remains the same to this day. To take part, you simply count the birds in your garden for an hour, note down the highest number of individuals of each species you see at any one time, then send in your results to the RSPB. The event has proved hugely popular in the three decades of its existence, and the number of participants continues to increase each year – almost 400,000 individuals took part in the 2008 survey.

The event takes place in winter, which is one of the best times to record garden birds because of the large numbers seeking food and shelter on our doorsteps.

Once the results are in, the RSPB analyses them at a national and regional level to find out about garden birds in the UK. Looking at the results year by year enables the RSPB to monitor garden birds, their distribution, and any long-term trends in numbers. Over the past three decades participants in the Big Garden Birdwatch have made a significant contribution to monitoring the numbers of garden birds and have also helped highlight that some species are in need of help.

How to take part

The RSPB website contains everything you need to know to participate, including findings from past surveys. Taking part in the RSPB's Big Garden Birdwatch is fun and easy to do. The more people that take part, the wider the geographical coverage area will be – creating a more accurate picture of how our garden birds are faring

Counting birds
Record your results in a location where you have an unobstructed, calm, and clear view of the birds.

6 million birds were spotted in over **228,000** gardens in 2008.

Starling
With its iridescent feathers and distinctive bill, the Starling is an easy bird to spot in your garden.

in the UK. All you need to do is observe the birds in your garden or local park for a short time during the last weekend in January. Simply spend an hour counting the birds, recording the highest number of each species seen in your garden (not flying over) at any one time. It's important you don't count all the birds you see because some birds will return to your garden many times in the hour. For example, if you see the same Blue Tit 10 times you have not counted 10 Blue Tits.

If you don't have a garden you can take part in the event in a local park. Whichever location you choose, it's best to decide on a place where you can see the birds well and where you can sit quietly so they are not disturbed.

On the RSPB website you'll find a counting sheet, which you can download to help you keep track of how many birds you've seen. The sheet also provides images of the most common birds seen in gardens and space to cross off how many of each species you have seen together. You don't need to send this sheet back to the RSPB – it is just to help you record your findings. However, you can then submit your results online, using the survey form supplied. The results are published in March. **For more information visit www.rspb.org.uk/birdwatch**

What it tells us

During its three-decade history, the Big Garden Birdwatch survey has recorded huge declines in some of the country's most familiar birds. For example, since 1979, the number of House Sparrows counted has fallen by more than half, and the number of Starlings by over three quarters; since 2004 overall bird numbers have dropped by 5 per cent. However, the survey also provides positive information about our bird population – Chaffinches have increased by over 30 per cent

TOP TEN BIRDS 2008
House Sparrow
Starling
Blackbird
Blue Tit
Chaffinch
Woodpigeon
Collared Dove
Robin
Great Tit
Goldfinch

and Great Tits by more than 50 per cent since 1979; Goldfinch numbers are up 30 per cent since 2004, and Bramblings, Siskins, and Redpolls are all improving. This, and all the other data collected helps the RSPB prioritize its conservation work. In 2008, 72 different species of bird were recorded over the Birdwatch weekend, with Greenfinches, Dunnocks, Magpies, Long-tailed Tits, and Jackdaws just outside the top ten species (see p. 91). Encouragingly, Song Thrush numbers were up 80 per cent compared to the previous year. This was probably due to a warm, wet summer, making it easier for the birds to find slugs, snails, and worms to feed their young. The Big Garden Birdwatch survey also throws up surprises each year, and some unusual birds have been spotted in gardens, including Red Kites, Firecrests, Hawfinches, and Little Egrets.

About the RSPB

The Royal Society for the Protection of Birds (RSPB) was founded in 1889 to combat the trade in wild birds' plumes. Since then, the number of issues the society tackles has increased enormously and its membership has grown to more than one million members. The RSPB could not undertake its vital work to help wild birds and other wildlife without its supporters and members. Such strength of support has enabled the RSPB to grow into Europe's biggest conservation charity.

Birds and the habitats in which they live are under more pressure than ever before. The RSPB is involved in a huge range of issues that affect birds and wildlife, such as conserving and restoring important areas for wildlife across the UK – including managing more than 200 nature reserves, tackling wildlife crime,

Rarely spotted
With its orange crown and bright markings, the Firecrest is a distinctive, if seldom-seen garden bird.

working with decision makers and landowners, and sharing expertise and knowledge to help young and old enjoy the natural world.

The RSPB helps wild birds both in the UK and, increasingly, abroad through a global conservation partnership called BirdLife International. Projects include helping to save the world's albatrosses from extinction and stopping the illegal hunting of migratory birds in southern Europe.

You can support the RSPB in many ways, from becoming a member to making a donation and purchasing RSPB goods, including bird food, feeders, and nest boxes for your garden birds. Attend one of hundreds of RSPB events that take place all over the UK and join in the Society's Big Garden Birdwatch, Homes for Wildlife, and Feed The Birds Day. You can also volunteer with the RSPB or join a local group.

Red Kite
Once rare in the UK, this species has made an astonishing recovery.

For more information on the RSPB, its work and how to join, visit **www.rspb.org.uk**, telephone RSPB UK headquarters on 01767 680551, or write to The Lodge, Potton Road, Sandy, Bedfordshire SG19 2DL.

a million voices for nature

Index

A
anatomy 56–7
autumn 28–9
B
bacon rind 47
bathing 48–9
beaks 23, 57, 62
berries 35–7
binoculars 7, 66
bird-baths 48
bird cake 46
bird pudding 39
bird tables 40–1, 44
Blackbird 5, 75
 feathers 58–9
 nest boxes 50
 singing 12
 young birds 26
Blackcap 30, 78
Black-headed Gull 65
Blue Tit 81
 courtship 15
 feeding 4, 22, 40–1
 nest boxes 50–2
 nests 17
 singing 13
 territory 10–11
 wings 65
bones 56–7
Brambling 5, 30, 87
bread 39
breeding
 courtship 14–15
 eggs 18
 nests 16–17
Bullfinch 24, 89
Bunting, Reed 89
C
cake, feeding birds 47
Carrion Crow 84
cats 42, 44–5
Chaffinch 20, 27, 30, 86
chicks 18–19,
Chiffchaff 78
clutch size 18

Coal Tit 80
coconut 38
Collared Dove 19, 61,
 63, 71
colours 58–9
contour feathers 57
counting birds 67
courtship 14–15
Crow, carrion 84
D
Dove, Collared 19, 61,
 63, 71
Dunnock 61, 70, 74
 courtship 14
 feeding 41, 44
E
ears 57
eggs 18
eyes 57
F
feathers 57
 bathing 48–9
 colours and markings
 58–9
 identifying 59
 insulation 30–1
 moulting 28
 preening 57, 59
 in spring 24
 in summer 26
feeders 40–5
 bird tables 40–1
 ground feeders 41,
 hanging feeders 42
 siting 44–5
 specialist feeders 43
feeding 22–3, 36–7
 in autumn 28
 making food 46–7
 safety 26
 in spring 24
 in summer 26
 types of food 38–9
 in winter 30
feet 57
Fieldfare 5, 20, 30, 76
fighting 11
finches

beaks 23, 62
 feeding 43
 flocks 10
 skulls 62
 in winter 34
fledglings 19
flight 64–5
flight feathers 56
flocks 10, 28
Flycatcher, Spotted 50,
 52, 62
food see feeding
foraging 23
fruit 36–7, 47
G
Goldcrest 13, 28, 79
Goldfinch 28, 36,
 41, 58, 87
Great Spotted Woodpecker
 5, 19, 25, 52, 66–7, 72
Great Tit 81
Greenfinch 4, 6, 26, 48, 88
 nests 17
 plumage 58
 wings 64
Green Woodpecker 11,
 65, 72
Grey Heron 68
grooming 59
ground feeders 41
Gull, Black-headed 65
H
habitat, garden 34–5
hanging feeders 42
hatching 18
hearing 57
hoarding food 23
House Martin 5, 20, 24,
 26, 51
House Sparrow 5, 26,
 61, 86
hygiene
 bird tables 41
 feeders 42
 nest boxes 51
I
identifying birds 7, 55–65
incubation, eggs 18

J
Jackdaw 65, 83
Jay 23, 29, 49, 59, 82
K
Kestrel 65
L
Long-tailed Tit 79
M
Magpie 63, 83
markings 59
Marsh Tit 80
Martin, House 26
    migration, 5, 20, 24
    nest boxes 51
mealworms 38
migration 20–1, 24, 30, 64
Mistle Thrush 76
moulting 28
N
nest boxes 24
    cleaning 28
    making 52–3
    types of 50–1
nests 16–17, 34
Nuthatch 5, 6, 23, 51, 82
nuts 38–9
nyjer seed 43
O
Owl, Tawny 57, 71
    feathers 59
    flight 65
    nest boxes 51
    senses 57
    skulls 62
P
peanuts 38–9, 42
Pied Wagtail 24, 50, 73
Pigeons 61, 65, 70
plumage see feathers
predators 24, 26, 40, 44
preening 57, 59
ponds 35
R
record-keeping 7, 67
Redwing 5, 30, 77
Reed Bunting 89
rice, feeding birds 47
Robin 5, 60, 75

beak 63
    feathers 31, 56–7
    feeding 42, 47
    fledglings 19
    migration 20
    nest boxes 50
    plumage 58
    singing 13
    territory 10
Rock Dove 70
Rook 65, 83
RSPB 70–1
S
seeds
    hanging feeders 42
    natural food 35–7
    seed mixes 38–9
senses 57
shape, identifying birds 61
shelter 36
singing 12–13
Siskin 5, 30, 59, 88
size, identifying birds 60–1
skeleton 56–7
skulls 62
song posts 10, 13
Song Thrush 71
Sparrow, House 5,
        26, 61, 86
    beaks 62
    nest boxes 51–2
    nesting 18
    young birds 19
Sparrowhawk 44,
        60, 65, 69
Spotted Flycatcher 50,
        52, 62
spring 24–5
squirrels 41, 43
Starling 24, 85
    beak 62
    calls 13
    feathers 59
    feeding 35, 42
    flocks 10, 66
    migration 20–1
    nest boxes 52
    wings 65

summer 26–7
Swallow 21, 23, 63
Swift 66
    feeding 23
    identifying 61
    migration 5, 20, 24
    nest boxes 51
    wings 64–5
T
tails 63
Tawny Owl 51, 57, 59, 62,
        65, 71
territory 10–11
Thrush 20, 34–5, 61–2
    Mistle 16–17, 76
    Song 12–13, 22, 41, 77
Tits 10, 61–2, 64
    Coal 23, 28, 51–2, 80
    Great 10–11, 40–1,
        51–2, 81
    Long-tailed 17, 63, 79
Marsh 80
    see also Blue Tit
trees 36
W
Wagtail, Pied 24, 50, 73
warblers 62
watching birds 66–7
water 26, 30, 48–9
wings
    flight feathers 56
    shape 64–5
winter 30–1
Woodpecker 62, 65
    Great Spotted 5,
        19, 25, 52, 66–7, 72
    Green 11, 65, 72
Woodpigeon 5, 19, 70
Wren 74
    nest boxes 50
    plumage 58
    singing 13
    tails 63
    wings 64

Acknowledgments

Dorling Kindersley would like to thank Ben Hoare for additional editing and proofreading, Hilary Bird for indexing, and Tamlyn Calitz and Jaime Tenreiro for assistance with the project.

The publisher would like to thank the following for their kind permission to reproduce their photographs:

(Key: a-above; b-below/bottom; c-centre; l-left; r-right; t-top)

Alamy Images: blickwinkel 15, 64; Les Borg 29; Andrew Darrington 25, 47; Martin Fowler 75; Juniors Bildarchiv 1; Mike Lane 76; Renee Morris 2

Aquila Wildlife Images: Mike Wilkes 88tr

R.J. Chandler: 74bl

David Cottridge: 72cla

Corbis: Eric and David Hosking 75crb; David Cottridge: 72cla

DK Images: Kim Taylor 10, 13br, 16-17, 18t, 20, 22, 39t, 59t, 60b, 63

Paul Doherty: 83br

Göran Ekström: 83tl

FLPA: 79cb; Martin B Withers 71cr

Chris Gomersall Photography: 68br, 68crb, 70ca, 70clb, 71tl, 72cra, 73c, 74clb, 75cra, 75tr, 76crb, 77cra, 81tl, 82crb, 83ca, 84br, 84crb, 84tl, 84tr, 85bl, 85c, 86clb, 86cr, 86cra, 86tl, 88clb, 88fbr, 88tl

Mark Hamblin: 69fbl, 71br, 72br, 74crb, 76bl, 81fcra, 86fbl, 89br, 89cb, 89cla, 89cra, 89fcla

Chris Knights: 87crb, 87tl

Mike Lane: 73bl, 75cb, 75clb, 76ca, 76cra, 77ca, 78tr, 79br, 80ca, 87fcra, 89bl

Tim Loseby: 73clb

George McCarthy: 82cra

Alan Petty: 70bl

Photolibrary: OSF / Paulo de Olive 71clb

rspb-images.com: 4, 7tl, 40bl, 4 43br, 50t, 51tr; Nigel Blake 13tr; Brooks 21, 72clb, 75br (immature), Laurie Campbell 12; Geoff Dore 5 Gerald Downey 63t; Bob Glover 1 32-33, 49, 50b, 69tl, 85tl; Danny Green 93tr; Mark Hamblin 69cr, 72crb, 77crb, 81br, 82clb, 89tr; Tony Hamblin 21b, 79tr; Andy Hay 11br; Robert Horn Malcolm Hunt 79ca; ; Ray Kenn David Kjaer 19, 69bl, 81cr, 92-93; Steve Knell 71bl; Chris Knights 73tr; Mike Lane 84cla, 88br; Gordon Langsbury 75cla; John Lawton Roberts 72tl, Mike McKavett 74tl; Philip Newman 77tr, Bill Paton 79crb, 83clb; Mike Read 48bl; David Tipling 8-9; Maurice Walker 80bc; Roger Wilmshurst 27

Roger Tidman: 68bl, 70br, 70tr, 71cra, 76cb, 78bc, 78br, 78ca, 78cra, 81ca, 81crb, 82tl, 85bc, 86br, 86c, 87br, 88fcla;

Colin Varndell: 78crb, 80crb

Roger Wilmshurst: 83crb, 87cb

Steve Young: 73fclb, 74cla, 79cla, 83cra, 89crb

Jacket images: Front: **Alamy Images:** Pictorial Press Ltd. Spine: **Alamy Images:** Pictorial Press Ltd. Back: **rspb-images:** Laurie Campbell clb; Andy Ray br; Ray Kennedy bl,tl; Chris Knights clb.

All other images © Dorling Kindersley For further information see: **www.dkimages.com**